Essential Design for
Web Professionals

ISBN 0-13-032161-3

90000

9 780130 321619

- *Essential Design for Web Professionals*
  Charles Lyons

- *Essential Flash 5 for Web Professionals*
  Lynn Kyle

- *Essential Flash 4 for Web Professionals*
  Lynn Kyle

- *Essential ASP for Web Professionals*
  Elijah Lovejoy

- *Essential PHP for Web Professionals*
  Christopher Cosentino

- *Essential CSS & DHTML for Web Professionals*
  Dan Livingston and Micah Brown

- *Essential JavaScript™ for Web Professionals*
  Dan Barrett, Dan Livingston, and Micah Brown

- *Essential Perl 5 for Web Professionals*
  Micah Brown, Chris Bellow, and Dan Livingston

- *Essential Photoshop® 5 for Web Professionals*
  Brad Eigen, Dan Livingston, and Micah Brown

Essential Design for Web Professionals

Charles J. Lyons

Micah Brown
Series Editor

Prentice Hall PTR
Upper Saddle River, NJ 07458
www.phptr.com

Library of Congress Cataloging-in-Publication Data

Lyons, Charles J.
    Essential design for web professionals / Charles J. Lyons.
        p. cm.
    Includes bibliographical references and index.
    ISBN 0-13-032161-3
        1. Web site development. 2. Web sites—Design.   I. Title.

TK5105.888.L98 2001
005.7'2—dc21

                                                    00-047879

Editorial/Production Supervision: Jan H. Schwartz
Acquisitions Editor: Karen McLean
Cover Design Director: Jerry Votta
Cover Design: Nina Scuderi
Manufacturing Manager: Alexis R. Heydt
Marketing Manager: Kate Hargett
Editorial Assistant: Rick Winkler
Art Director: Gail Cocker-Bogusz
Series Interior Design: Meg VanArsdale

© 2001 Prentice Hall PTR
Prentice-Hall, Inc.
Upper Saddle River, NJ 07458

Prentice Hall books are widely used by corporations and
government agencies for training, marketing, and resale.

The publisher offers discounts on this book when ordered in bulk quantities.
For more information, contact: Corporate Sales Department, Phone: 800-382-3419;
Fax: 201-236-7141; E-mail: corpsales@prenhall.com; or write:
Prentice Hall PTR, Corp. Sales Dept., One Lake Street, Upper Saddle River, NJ 07458.

Printed in the United States of America
10   9   8   7   6   5   4   3   2   1

ISBN 0-13-032161-3

Prentice-Hall International (UK) Limited, *London*
Prentice-Hall of Australia Pty. Limited, *Sydney*
Prentice-Hall Canada Inc., *Toronto*
Prentice-Hall Hispanoamericana, S.A., *Mexico*
Prentice-Hall of India Private Limited, *New Delhi*
Prentice-Hall of Japan, Inc., *Tokyo*
Pearson Education Asia Pte. Ltd.
Editora Prentice-Hall do Brasil, Ltda., *Rio de Janeiro*

*This book is dedicated to my wife, Patricia; to my son Robert,
his wife Lisa, their children and my grandchildren Clark and Jack;
to my daughter Mary Pat and her husband John;
to my daughter Carol, her husband Chris, their children and
my grandchildren Sean, Kevin, and Shannon; to my son Michael;
and to the memory of my parents, Charles James Lyons and
Anne Veronica Donovan Lyons.*

Contents

Introduction

When I decided to write this book, it was my intention to provide to Web professionals a cogent and defendable methodology for developing Web sites. For years, I have seen both systems and Web sites developed in an undisciplined manner. What results is a system or Web site for which a great deal of retrofitting and reengineering is necessary. Retrofitting is expensive and its necessity is the result of not taking a thorough and disciplined approach to developing the Web site.

The methodology suggested herein is based upon sound systems engineering principles. The approach is to perform a thorough and complete requirements analysis up front. A solid analysis provides the foundation for designing a Web site that will meet the users' needs each and every time. A successful Web site will also be easy to maintain, since major blocks of thought are not left out. While revisions are needed, they will be more related to the business needs and exigencies than to faulty, premature design.

Throughout this book, there are images that are worth viewing in color. At various points in the text, you will be prompted to visit a Web site, where color versions of the images are shown.

Acknowledgments

I would like to acknowledge the following people for their contributions and inspiration: Bill Harrod, Vice President, Lucent Technologies' Learning and Performance Center, for creating and sustaining a high-performance organization; Chuck Kirschenmann, Director, Learning and Performance Center, for his leadership and direction; Terry Westermann, my coach, and Lilliam Valdes-Diaz, my former coach, for encouraging me to write this book; Sharmila R. Deshpande, a student of mine who has made valuable contributions to this book; and to Robert Lyons of Unidex, Inc. for his expertise and assistance in XML.

About the Author

Charles J. Lyons is currently the president and founder of Tektrain, Inc., providers of world-class technical training. Prior to that, he was a Member of the Technical Staff at Lucent Technologies' Learning and Performance Center, where he was responsible for the development and delivery of usability engineering, Web development, rapid prototyping, and technical documentation training. Charlie also developed and maintained the Learning and Performance Center's Internal Human Factors Curriculum Web site.

Charlie joined AT&T in 1970, and was responsible for developing and deploying information systems standards to various organizations within AT&T. In 1980, he moved to AT&T's Technical Education Center, where he developed and taught a variety of human factors, systems analysis, and technical writing courses. In 1996, when Lucent Technologies was divested from AT&T, Charlie continued to develop and teach in Lucent Technologies' Learning and Performance Center. During this time, he delivered training via distance learning through video conferencing and the Lucent intranet.

Charlie is a Certified Technical Trainer (CTT) and a Certified Computer Professional (CCP). An author of several articles and a frequent conference speaker, he was awarded the Most Inspirational Speaker award at Lucent Technologies' Web Week '98. Charlie holds a Ph.D. in education, and in 1999, was inducted into the *International Who's Who in Information Technology*. In 2000, he was listed in *The International Executive Who's Who*.

You may reach Charlie Lyons at *cjlyons@tektrain.com* and visit the Tektrain, Inc. Web site at *http://www.tektrain.com*. A screen snapshot of the Tektrain Web site is shown below.

1 Introduction to Web Analysis and Design

IN THIS CHAPTER

- Web Design Difficulties
- Summary: Web Design Difficulties
- Transition to Analysis
- The Web Development Cycle
- Differences in GUI and Web Design
- The Prototyping Cycle
- Source of System Errors

Imagine you have been called into your boss's office. Your boss says, "We've just received a directive to develop a corporate Web site. It has to be done in one month and it has to be done right! No shortcuts and no quick and dirty approach that will lead to endless reengineering and retro-fitting. The directive indicates that the methodology used to develop the site must be as rigorous and thorough as that used to develop and deploy software systems. Our corporate Web standards group has mandated we use Macromedia Dreamweaver 3 as an implementation tool. Any questions?"

Don't panic! You will be able to develop, test, and implement the corporate Web site using a solid methodology. You will also be able to learn Dreamweaver 3 quickly so that you can use this powerful tool successfully. Let's get started with the basics!

◆ Web Design Difficulties

The Web presents unique design difficulties. These include

- too much information
- impatience of Web readers
- limits to short-term memory
- tendency to get lost
- reading from screens more difficult than paper

Too Much Information

The Web consists of volumes of information, which is sometimes disorganized and difficult to get through. In order to make any sense out of the information, the reader must often resort to trial and error to ferret out logic that should have been organized and made obvious by the author.

Impatience of Web Readers

Web pages can render slowly, causing the user endless frustration. Users will leave a Web site in about two to four seconds if they do not see something useful at the outset. Often, the reason for this quick exit is that the information is presented in a disorganized or confusing way.

Limits in Short-Term Memory

Coupled with user impatience, are limits in short-term memory (STM). STM is the throwaway memory that we use every day to function, and it is fragile. For example, suppose that you have just looked up a telephone number and are about to dial the phone. Someone comes into your office and asks, "Would you like to go to lunch?" It is likely that the phone number will pop out of your memory and you'll have to look it up again.

There are real limits to STM that are independent of culture, intelligence, and gender. Generally, people can handle about four to six items of information at one time. Presenting information into groups of four to six items is essential to enable readers to scan a Web page quickly and find information. Reading pages on the Web is slower than reading from a paper document.

Tendency to Get Lost

Web pages are not always well organized. Readers have difficulty, since they are often dealing with different formats.

With disciplined, logical thinking, a designer can build an interface that will guide users through a site so that every click adds value to the user's task. Links and navigation on a Web site should be intuitive; that is, the user should be able to use the site without having to resort to trial and error.

Reading from Screens More Difficult

For a variety of reasons, reading from screens is more difficult than reading from paper. Fonts are not as clear and crisp. Readers generally see one screen in front of them at one time. The space available to the designer is limited. Therefore, the designer must create an efficient and lean screen design that facilitates scanning and finding critical information. My experience is that continually reading from a screen is tiring, so keeping text short and lean should be an overall objective.

◆ Summary: Web Design Difficulties

We've seen that designing for the Web presents these challenges:

- too much information
- impatience of Web readers
- limits to short-term memory
- tendency to get lost
- reading from screens is slower and more difficult than reading from paper

As we said, there are solutions and this book will present them!

◆ Transition to Analysis

Web analysis and design is an iterative process. Through prototyping our Web site (including alternative designs), we can dramatically increase our odds of success. But to really achieve success, we need to employ a user-centered design,[1] which states that

- The user is the center of the design universe.
- Design decisions are made based on making the user's tasks easier.

Implementing this approach requires a thorough understanding of

- who the users are,
- what tasks they will be performing,
- how they will be using the Web site.

◆ The Web Development Cycle

Figure 1–1 shows the iterative nature of Web Development. We will first focus on conducting a thorough and complete analysis so that a clear set of requirements can be developed. Then, in Chapter 3, "Design," we will look at efficient ways to organize the navigation and content so that a user of our Web site will be able to access critical information, quickly and painlessly. In Chapter 4, "Implementation and Testing," we will use Macromedia Dreamweaver 3 to build the Web site. Then we will conduct usability tests to ensure that the Web site meets the needs of the users.

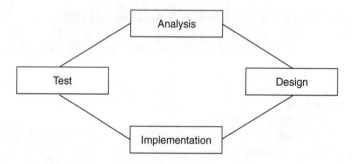

FIGURE 1–1 The Web development cycle.

◆ Differences in GUI and Web Design

A unique challenge in Web design is that the developer does not have full control over the final presentation of the site. Readers can resize windows and change default fonts and colors. Moreover, different hardware and software platforms render the same Web page differently.

◆ The Prototyping Cycle

Figure 1–2 shows the iterative nature of the prototyping cycle.

The prototyping cycle can be used throughout the Web development cycle. Early on, we can develop paper prototypes and show them to the user. This helps us to get inside the mind of the user better than if we just ask abstract questions. We can use Macromedia Dreamweaver 3 to build a quick prototype that provides some interactivity, which helps the user express his or her ideas more clearly.

So we see that a developer can build a prototype, test it with the user, modify the prototype based on the user's input, and continue this cycle, thereby helping to ensure a successful implementation. Additionally, the developer can test various prototype versions with the user and compare performance. For each alternative, how fast did the user perform and how many errors were made? In this way, the most efficacious alternative can be selected for further development. Prototyping is an excellent way to analyze and define the Web site's requirements.

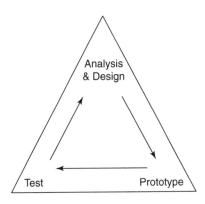

FIGURE 1–2 The prototyping cycle. (*Source:* Human Factors Curriculum, Learning and Performance Center, Lucent Technologies, 1999)

◆ Source of System Errors

For some time now, we have known where the source of system errors is in the systems development life cycle (SDLC). At least 60 to 80 percent of the errors in a system can be traced back to faulty requirements being developed in the requirements-definition phase. The remaining 20 to 40 percent of errors are attributable to all of the other phases combined.

It is imperative, therefore, that a thorough and rigorous analysis be performed to reveal the requirements of the Web site. Otherwise, the developers and programmers are set off on the wrong azimuth, and the eventual site implementation, while technically correct, bears little resemblance to the needs of the users, since these needs were not identified early on.

Notes

1. Human Factors Curriculum, Learning and Performance Center, Lucent Technologies, 1999.

2 Analysis

With our introductory chapter behind us, it is now time to focus on what can be the most important phase of the Web development cycle—Analysis. If a rigorous analysis of the site's purpose, audience, information needed, and activities to be performed is conducted, then the likelihood of a successful Web site is tremendously increased.

It is tempting to want to jump right in and start physical design using some tool, but that approach is more than likely to result in expensive retrofitting and reengineering.

7

◆ Analysis Steps

The analysis steps[1] in building a Web site are

- Determine the goals and success criteria for your Web site.
- Determine your audience and how they will use the Web site.
- Determine and organize information topics.
- Analyze constraints and plan for their resolution.
- Modify the goals, success criteria, and information, based upon constraints.

Each of these steps will be covered in detail, using Shelley Biotechnologies as a case study. A scenario of Shelley Biotechnologies follows.

◆ Shelley Biotechnologies

Shelley's Mission

Shelley Biotechnologies' mission is to become the definitive source of DNA interactions under thornachloride. Shelley also has a GenLab, which is ushering in a new age in genetic research, as well as in related biological and medical research. Research is applied also to the development of software tools that provide the ability to view, browse, and analyze research data in an integrated way to facilitate discovery. Shelley offers a variety of services to customers to assist in the analysis and interpretation of the data. Currently, Shelley is developing new databases and services in the emerging field of genetics. These databases of information will enable researchers throughout the world to further their research and their understanding of the biological world.

About Shelley Biotechnologies

Shelley Biotechnologies is a global company with offices and research facilities in the United States, Canada, London, Singapore, and India. Shelley provides products and services spanning the field of genetics. It provides up-to-date information on genetic news and also provides training on its products.

Maurice E. Shelley, Ph.D., a researcher and educator, founded Shelley Biotechnologies five years ago. Dr. Shelley opened the first facility in Princeton, New Jersey, and the company quickly grew to its present size. Shelley employs 6,000 researchers and staff personnel throughout the world.

Need for a Web Site

Dr. Shelley, the CEO, has made it clear that the company needs a corporate Web site. As a researcher and as CEO, Dr. Shelley has incredibly high standards. His goal is to make the company a world leader in genetic research. Dr. Shelley's standards and expectations for the corporate Web site are no less rigorous. Within Shelley, speed is a shared value and customer satisfaction an obsession.

Specifications for the Web Site

As scientists, Dr. Shelley and his management team have set down rigorous specifications for their site. These specifications are detailed in this and succeeding chapters, and form the basis for the execution of the Web analysis and design methodology presented in this book.

◆ Determining the Goals of Your Site

To get the best return for a Web site, you must be specific and knowledgeable about what you are trying to accomplish. Targeting your Web site goals[2] is probably the most important step in developing a Web site. Everything that follows in analysis and design depends on a good goals statement.

Businesses and organizations typically want to get on the Web for a combination of the following reasons:

- provide research information
- global presence
- provide information regarding products and services
- enable customers to provide feedback and information
- provide online ordering of products and services
- internally, as a repository for company policies, documentation, and correspondence
- provide an extranet where outside organizations can access a portion of the company's intranet, for example, to interact for e-commerce purposes

Primary and Secondary Goals

Once you give these questions some thought, you may find that you have several goals. You may want to divide these into primary and secondary goals,[3] considering the following.

- What is going to give you the best return on investment?
- What is going to generate results that are of interest to
  - your shareholders?
  - your customers?

Here are some examples of Web site goals.

- Promote a product or service
- Tell customers about my company
- Provide a presence on the Internet
- Solicit feedback from customers

◆ Determining the Success Criteria for Your Web Site

In the next step, you want to give yourself some specific, quantifiable results with which to measure your success.[4] Here are some questions that will help:

- How many users visit your Web site per day or per week?
- How long do your users stay at your site?
- What do your users do while visiting your Web site?
- How many pages or resources do your users use or visit during a typical session?
- How often do your users come back to visit your site?
- How can you measure the positive contribution of the Web site on the bottom line of your business?

◆ Determining the Audience and How They Will Use the Web Site

Next we need to determine our audience and how they will use the Web site. Some questions to consider are

- Who is your audience?
- What will your audience want?
- What are the information needs of your audience?
- Can competitors access your site?

Web Site Audience Analysis

OVERVIEW

Now that the audience has been determined, the next step is to analyze each audience[5] along the following criteria:

- interests, needs, skills, capabilities, and assumptions
- platform, browser, application connection speed, and degree of Net savvy and experience
- platform descriptions to include make, models, RAM, hard drives, CD-ROM, and other equipment

◆ Information Topics

Determining Information Topics

As part of your logical analysis, it is important to determine all of the content your site will need. The content should be at the topic level.[6] Examples of information topics include

- location of the company
- history of the company
- products
- services

Organizing Information Topics into Categories

The next step is to organize the information topics into categories, or families, of information. Let us assume that the design team has arrived at the following categories:

- About Shelley
- Common Good Projects
- Services
- Training
- Genetic News

Status of Information Topics

It is useful to consider each information topic in terms of the status of the underlying information.[7] Table 2–1 shows a sample list of information topics and an example of how to show the status for each.

TABLE 2-1 Status of Information Topics

Information Topic	Status of Information
Locations	Need to scan maps.
Shelley Description and Services	Text written. Need new pictures.
Company Policies	Basic text written. Need to add information regarding firewall security.
Genetic News	Need to develop. Need map/pictures.
How to Contact Shelley	Need to develop online form.

◆ Information Taxonomy

After all information items have been identified and categorized, they are arranged into a taxonomy, or hierarchy. This is a logical analysis breakdown of information. Figure 2–1 shows an information taxonomy for Shelley Biotechnologies.

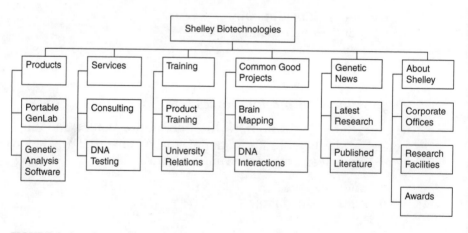

FIGURE 2-1 Information taxonomy for Shelley Biotechnologies.

◆ Task Analysis

Rationale

Another excellent methodology that can be employed is task analysis. Task analysis has a rich history of providing a way to show the task-flow for human activities. If no task analysis is done, it is quite likely that the Web screens may render in a manner that does not match the sequence of steps that the user follows.

For example, imagine that a customer has telephoned Shelley Biotechnologies to request information on training courses. If no task analysis were performed in the design of the system, the screens would likely render in a random fashion, or according to how the designer arranged them. This would not only confuse the Shelley Biotechnologies' customer service representative, but the customer as well. The customer service representative would have to use trial and error to handle the customer's request. Trial and error is expensive, non-value added, and will likely result in errors.

For Shelley Biotechnologies

For Shelley Biotechnologies, a task analysis could determine a likely sequence in which the customer service representative might navigate the site. The navigation of the site could then be optimized to ensure an intuitive experience for the customer service representative and for the customer as well. Figure 2–2 shows an initial task-flow for Shelley.

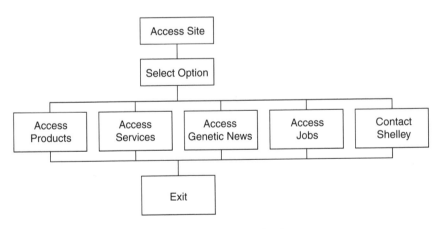

FIGURE 2–2 Initial task flow for Shelley Biotechnologies.

◆ Web Site Constraints

Overview

Before going further with our analysis, it is wise to consider what constraints[8] might exist that could affect the performance and usability of Shelley Biotechnologies' Web site. A constraint is a stumbling block, or obstacle, that needs to be addressed in order for the Web site to be successful. For example, if a user has a text-only browser, we will have to consider alternatives to showing pictures on our site.

Constraints for Shelley Biotechnologies

We need to identify what constraints exist for Shelley. Examples of constraints include:

- low bandwidth
- users with character-based browsers
- inability to show robust multimedia due to current bandwidths and technology

After we identify the constraints, we use a scale of high (H), medium (M), and low (L) to prioritize the constraints. It is important to have a mix and match of high, medium, and low. If all or most constraints are rated high, for example, we have not really separated our thinking. A constraint that is rated low can be incredibly important. However, it is less important than one rated high or medium.

We then record solutions for each constraint, determine the responsible person who will implement the solutions, and determine the date by which the resolutions should be implemented. Table 2–2 shows the constraints and their resolutions for Shelley Biotechnologies.

TABLE 2–2 Constraints for Shelley Biotechnologies

Constraint	Priority	Resolution	Responsible Person	Target Date
Bandwidth vs. mandate for graphics and multimedia	H	Use Macromedia Flash 5; employs vector graphics, which are less demanding on resources.	P. Silver	4/1
Lack of staff knowledge of HTML and multimedia	M	Use Macromedia Dreamweaver 3 & Flash 5; give staff copies of *Essential Series* books for each.	J. Larcher	2/1
Globalization requirement vs. time and cost	L	Begin with version for USA and Europe. Add other countries and locations over time.	R. Quigley	3/1

(*Source:* Information Mapping, Inc., Internal Course Materials, 1996)

◆ Modifying Web Site to Reflect Constraints

Based upon the constraints[9] identified above, it may be necessary to go back and modify the initial goals, success criteria, and information topics for the Web site. Such modifications could have an impact on the Web project schedule. In this particular case, it does not appear that any modifications to our analysis so far are needed.

◆ Transition to Design

In Chapter 2, we have been discussing *analysis*, which is intended to separate differences. In our information taxonomy, we separated our information into distinctive categories. Within each category, we made sure that we had all the information topics we needed. The representation of these information topics was thorough, but not efficient. Efficiency is a design concept.

For example, in analysis, we separated training into product training and university relations. This separation was thorough, but not efficient. The separation was done to be sure that we had not forgotten anything.

In Chapter 3, "Design," we will consider efficiency. We will pull together similarities of information that were separated in analysis and integrate similar topics into an efficient user interface. For example, the components of training will be pulled together in design. Any commonalities regarding product training and university training will be stated up front for efficiency. Product training and university training will be presented in a consistent way to maximize efficiency and enhance user access and readability.

In Chapter 3, we will develop a Navigation Flowchart. The Navigation Flowchart is physical, not logical, and will show the navigation paths that our Web visitor will follow when visiting Shelley Biotechnologies. By contrast, the information taxonomy developed in analysis is logical. No navigation paths or logical precedence are implied.

Notes

1. Information Mapping, Inc., Internal Course Materials, 1996 (Information Mapping is a registered trademark of Information Mapping, Inc.).

2. DiNucci, Darcy, et al., Maria Giudice, and Lynne Stiles, *Elements of Web Design*, 2d ed. (Berkeley, Calif.: Peachpit Press, 1998), 38–41.
3. Ibid., 41.
4. Human Factors Curriculum, Learning and Performance Center, Lucent Technologies, 1999.
5. DiNucci, Darcy, Maria Giudice, and Lynne Stiles, et al., *Elements of Web Design*, 2d ed. (Berkeley, Calif.: Peachpit Press, 1998) 41.
6. Information Mapping, Inc., Internal Course Materials, 1996.
7. Ibid.
8. Ibid.
9. Ibid.

3 Design

IN THIS CHAPTER

- Design Steps
- Conceptual Model
- General Design Principles
- Navigation Questions
- Fundamental Principles of Web Design
- Fundamental Principles Applied to Architecture and Navigation
- Subphases of Design
- Navigation Design
- Information Structure
- Content Design
- Fundamental Principles Applied to Content
- Prototyping

Now that we have covered analysis, let us focus on design. Remember we said that thoroughness is an analysis concept and efficiency a design concept. The thoroughness of our analysis makes our design much easier. We can now focus on the most efficient and effective design of navigation and content, confident that nothing has been overlooked.

◆ Design Steps

The steps to be followed in designing a Web site follow. As with the analysis steps, the design steps are iterative.

- Determine the conceptual model for the Web site.
- Build a navigation flowchart showing the organization and navigational paths of the Web site.
- Build or update the prototype(s).

These steps will be covered in detail throughout this chapter.

◆ Conceptual Model

A conceptual model, or metaphor, is a method used to represent the essence, theme, and style of the Web site. For example, for an audience of engineers, the use of diagrams would be an appropriate model. The conceptual model must match the background of the user.

Imagine a nurse in a hospital who is being shown the latest Web interface system to be used to interact with doctors. The demonstrator of the system says to the nurse, "As you can see, this system has a great desktop metaphor." The nurse's eyes glaze over. He hasn't a clue what the demonstrator is talking about. The demonstrator of the system senses this and says, "How about if we showed a nursing station as a metaphor for the system?" The nurse responds, "That's great. Now I understand what you mean."

By the way, a simple paper prototype can easily determine whether the conceptual model or metaphor is appropriate.

◆ General Design Principles

User-Centered Design

User-centered design involves early and continuous focus on the users. We need to know our users, and we need to perform a task analysis. We also need to develop testable goals and conduct early and continuous user testing, which can be achieved through simulations, prototypes, and mockups.

Design is iterative. When we find problems, we need to have a willingness and ability to change.

A Team Sport

The design of Web sites requires a variety of skills not often found in one person. In designing our Web site, we need expertise in areas that include programming (Java, Perl, etc.), human factors or usability engineering, graphic design, videography (if multimedia is involved), and Web site server expertise.

While it can happen, it is extremely rare to find all of these skills in one person. There are those Renaissance people who are multidimensional and have many diverse skills. But as in the field of medicine, the design of sophisticated Web sites, which may include e-commerce, is likely to be more effective using specialists who are expert in particular disciplines.

Globalization

In design, we need to consider a variety of audience skills and preferences. Among our users, there is likely to be a great variety of technology platforms with a great variety of operating systems and software. These hardware/software platforms can be so varied that we need to be aware of the problems this variety can present to our design and implementation.

We also need to consider the diversity of the context in which different audience's view information. With a wide global audience, it is not very likely that one contextual representation of a Web site will do the trick. We may need to have different interfaces for these audiences. For example, the Chinese language has over 30,000 characters, while the Western alphabet has only 26. Moreover, Chinese characters are generally larger than Western characters. The same Web screen layout is not likely to work in this case. In other cultures, for example, in Saudi Arabia, text is read right to left. These complexities of content representation may demand a choice of different Web screen representations based upon a particular culture and country.

In addition, the context in which different cultures perceive the same information can vary greatly.

Compromise

It is not a perfect world and so design must involve compromising with the users at some level. For example, a client is implementing a system in China. The users absolutely insist on a lot of animated movement on the screen. This flies in the face of the principle of avoiding gratuitous or nonessential animation. The user in China may have numerous reasons for insisting on animation instead of a text-based approach. Experience has shown that younger users can tolerate movement much better than older users, and indeed, they expect it. This approach could have a negative effect on performance, since animation involves greater use of resources and can tax bandwidth. In this case, the use of Macromedia's Flash 5 would enable the use of vector graphics, which are stored as mathematical formulas. By avoiding raster graphics, which consume a lot of storage and memory, the likelihood of poorer performance due to animation can be mitigated.

Prototyping to Success

From the very beginning of our Web site development effort, we can develop a prototype, test it, redesign it based on user input, change the prototype, retest it, and continue this process until the users' information needs are satisfied. We can also prototype two or three design alternatives and show them to users to determine which is preferred. We can run a usability test on each of the two or three designs, and determine which is more efficacious in terms of performance, i.e., speed and accuracy.

Effective Standards and Collaboration

With Macromedia Dreamweaver 3, we can set up templates. We can establish style guides and specific conventions that the project team can agree to. The check in/check out feature of Dreamweaver 3 enables effective collaboration, since sections that are being modified are highlighted for everyone to see.

Avoid Bleeding-Edge Technology

There is an adage in medicine that says that a physician should not be the first to prescribe a new medicine and should not be the last to let go of an old one. The same holds true when choosing tools. New software can be buggy. If you have a software development tool that will meet the project development needs and is likely to be around for a while, you may be better off using that software tool than bringing in the latest, esoteric software that promises the world. Let other people and other companies work with the latest software, and only move to it when it will add value to your project effort without any danger of damaging it.

When designing, keep in mind what your tools can and cannot do. Do not promise the user something that your tools will not allow you to do. Keep in mind how much the project is costing and what time constraints you are facing.

Also, remember the capabilities of your staff. If you do not have robust programming expertise, you are better off designing within the framework of the staff's capabilities, as long as the product will meet the users' needs. A project with a tight deadline where there is not a lot of slack time is not the venue in which to give your staff stretch goals or tasks that are clearly beyond their expertise. If you do, you may miss the project implementation deadline and/or deliver a product that does not meet users' expectations.

User Support

Remember that the Web site you are developing should support your users in the tasks they are performing. We need to consider the users' tasks in the context of

- Specific steps they will be following for each task
- Requisite skills and knowledge they need for successful performance

Minimalist Approach

Less is more. Sometimes, we are tempted to put bells and whistles into a Web page that are not relevant to the tasks the user is performing. Web sites that are too complicated for their intended use will likely frustrate the user and make your site maintenance a nightmare. Sophistication can add value, but unnecessary bells and whistles to showcase the ability to use a particular piece of software should be avoided.

Remember, your Web site has a goal or purpose, and its intent is normally to support people in the performance of their job tasks. Of course, there are entertainment sites where streaming audio, video, and other effects are what the audience expects. But if you are designing for business, keep it simple. If a text hyperlink will do the job, why not use it rather than an image hyperlink, which takes up more memory and storage.

Focus on Monochrome First

Your design will go more smoothly if you focus on the right navigation and content, and think about color at little later. There is a temptation to jump right in with snazzy colors to jazz things up. But remember that only certain foreground colors go with certain background colors. Overall, you want to achieve the best contrast in color, particularly with regard to text. Black text on an off-white or bone-white background is the best contrast, and hence your text will be more readable.

Of course, if you have templates and colors preselected, then certainly follow these standards. The idea here is not to get carried away with color too early. If, on the other hand, certain colors come to you, then write them down for later use. Keep in mind that certain colors have unique meanings in different cultures, and a particular color in a given use could even be considered inappropriate by a particular culture.

Set Measurable Usability Goals

Usability goals are the criteria that we are going to use to measure how fast someone can use our Web site and how few errors they make. A usability goal should be

- measurable
- specific
- realistic

Let us consider this goal: *the user will enter two transactions in an appropriate amount of time.* This is not a measurable goal. An "appropriate amount of time" is "fuzzy." What is appropriate to one person may not be appropriate to another. So if we are specific and state our goal as: *the user will be able to enter two transactions in three minutes, with 99 percent accuracy,* we are getting a little closer to measurability. However we need to define 99 percent accuracy. Does it mean that one typo (representing a 1 percent error) is okay? As you can see, we must be rigorous in how we define our usability goals.

And finally, our goals must be realistic, or attainable. If we set them too high, say 20 transactions in 3.5 minutes, we are being unrealistic. Even the best performer couldn't meet that goal.

Here are some examples of usability goals.

- The user will be able to unpack the computer, complete the installation, and boot the computer using the procedure job aid in 45 minutes.
- The service clerk will input 10 service orders in 15 minutes, with no errors.

- The Web user will be able to find the credit policy on Site X within 30 seconds.
- The Web user will be able to locate the specifications for the X32 Printer within 10 seconds.

◆ Navigation Questions

At any point, any reader of a Web site must be able to answer these questions.[1]

- Where am I?
- Where can I go?
- How can I get there?
- How can I get back?

People have been "navigating" through regular books for years. They can mark pages, access the table of contents, browse through the index, and flip to their favorite passages with ease. They are comfortable with the look and feel of a book and with reading crisp, black print on white paper.

However, on the Web, all readers have in front of them is a single screen with limited space. Consequently, given our perceptual and short-term memory limits, navigating the reader through the site becomes problematic. The chunking limit on the Web is four to six items of information. Moreover, people want to scan, not read, on the Web. Also, the resolution on the best monitors is poor compared with print on paper. Fonts render differently, depending on the hardware and software used. Since readers can resize their windows, hyperlinks may be less obvious.

Our challenge is to build an intuitive site where the reader can easily navigate simply by doing what comes naturally.

◆ Fundamental Principles of Web Design

Overview

Aside from all the sophisticated techniques one hears about in reference to Web design, there are four fundamental principles that are the underpinnings for both navigation and content design on the Web. These principles are so fundamental that failure to include them in analysis and design can render a site unfit for human consumption, notwithstanding the implementation of so-called sophisticated and advanced techniques.

These principles[2] are:

- Chunking
- Relevance
- Labeling
- Consistency

Principles Defined

Table 3-1 shows each principle and its definition.[3]

TABLE 3–1 Principles Defined

Principle	Definition
Chunking	Group information into small chunks of 4 to 6 items, following the online chunking limit of 5 plus or minus 1.
Relevance	Include in the chunk only those things that are the same. Exclude irrelevancies.
Labeling	Label each chunk.
Consistency	Present information in a consistent way, with no differences that do not make a difference.

◆ Fundamental Principles Applied to Architecture and Navigation

Table 3-2 shows how the principles can be applied to a Web site's architecture and navigational structure.

TABLE 3–2 Principles Applied to Architecture and Navigation

Principle	Applied to Web Site's Architecture and Navigational Structure
Chunking	• Make sure that your site's visible structure and navigation paths conform to the perceptual and short-term limits of humans. • Organize your site into chunks that are visible.
Relevance	• The parts, or chunks, of your site should each contain only those things that are relevant to that chunk or part. • Irrelevancies should be moved elsewhere or deleted.

(continued)

TABLE 3–2 *(Continued)*

Principle	Applied to Web Site's Architecture and Navigational Structure
Labeling	• Use labeling to make the architecture of your site obvious and intuitive to the reader. • Never have any information, links, or navigation paths that are not specifically labeled. • Avoid labels like back, next, up, down. Depending on page context and frame use, these types of labels can cause the reader to get lost. • Navigation can be assisted not only by software tools such as icons and buttons, but also by the nature and placement of information on your pages.

Consistency	• Use consistent navigation, e.g., a Help button shown the same size and in the same location on all Web pages in the site.
	• Use a given widget consistently. For example,
	  • Use hyperlink words for the user to obtain a pop-up window for a definition.
	  • Use buttons for Help wherever Help appears.
	  • We are not talking about mindless consistency. Any differences in navigation should be because the nature of the navigation is different. In other words, *all differences should be for a reason.* There should be no differences that do not make a difference.
	• Where a difference has a reason, your user will likely recognize the rationale for your choice.
	• Where you have a difference on a whim with no logical reason your reader will become frustrated and forced to use trial and error, or will exit the site in about three or four seconds. You as the writer will lose credibility fast.

◆ Subphases of Design

Design can be broken down into two subphases.

- Navigation design
- Content design

◆ Navigation Design

Navigation Flowchart

In Web site design, building a navigation flowchart enables the designer to get a picture of the architecture of the site and of the various paths that the user could take to navigate through the site.

Previously, we developed an information taxonomy, showing the logical breakdown of the information for a site. This information taxonomy was an *analysis* tool used for separating out all differences. The navigation flow chart *is* a *design* tool used to integrate all the similarities.

If a thorough information taxonomy has been developed, it can be easily converted into a navigation flowchart. Figure 3–1 shows a navigation flowchart for Shelley Biotechnologies.

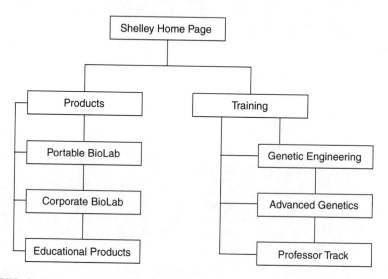

FIGURE3–1 Navigation flowchart for Shelley Biotechnologies.

◆ Information Structure

Need for Structure

Users sometimes feel helpless clicking from page to page. A good designer will present the user with a structured site and good navigational controls to move within it.

In order to accomplish this, the designer must

- build an intuitive site structure.
- make the structure visible to the user, even if the structure seems intuitive.
- give users location information so they know where they are and where they can go.

- present the user with clear, consistent navigational methods.

Web Information Structure

It is important to think about the ways in which information can be organized for the Web. This organization can also be a factor in the navigational layout of the pages on a Web site. The organization of information[4] on the Web can be

- Sequential
- Hierarchical
- Associative
- Combination of the above

SEQUENTIAL STRUCTURE

The sequential structure is the one most familiar to many users. Examples of sequential structures include

- Step-by-step procedures
- Process flows
- Depictions of events in time

HIERARCHICAL STRUCTURE

The most common example of a hierarchical structure is a company organization chart.[5] A common use of the hierarchical structure on Web pages involves having a home page with menu hyperlinks to lower levels of detail on succeeding pages.

ASSOCIATIVE STRUCTURE

An associative structure involves nonlinear navigation. This could be a hyperlink to a term in a glossary, or the retrieval of a circuit diagram from a database. Associative, or nonlinear, navigation fundamentally is any navigation that is not sequential or hierarchical. Navigation in an associative structure can be accomplished through full word or keyword searches as well.[6]

COMBINATION STRUCTURES

At times, we see combinations of structures in a Web site. For example, there could be a menu (hierarchical), which is in a certain sequence (order of importance), with a hyperlink in one of the menu items, which could lead to a definition of a term (associative).

How to Apply Information Structures

It is important to realize that we use the sequential, hierarchical, and associative structures as sets of ideas to help us think about Web site content structure. We do not have to zealously and rigorously force our information into these structures.

◆ Content Design

Introduction

Now that we have discussed navigation and navigation design, let us turn our attention to content design.

Content Types: Overview

It is useful to think of information as categorized into different content types. This helps us to be consistent in the way we present similar information throughout a Web site. Information can be broken down into the following categories:[7]

- Facts
- Concepts
- Procedures
- Processes
- Principles
- Structure

To demonstrate the usefulness of content types, let us consider two examples of categories of information that we would like to portray. The first category is concept, where we want to define a term. The second is procedure, where we want to delineate step-by-step instructions. Different presentations are used for each.

Defining a term, for example, pencil, might be best done as follows:

Definition: Pencil

A **pencil** is a writing instrument that is handheld, cylindrical in shape, and contains graphite.

On the other hand, if we want to specify step-by-step procedures to log onto a system, we would use a different presentation.

Procedure:

Follow these steps to log onto Genesis:

1. Type user name and press **ENTER**.
2. Type your password and press **ENTER**.
3. ....

Consistent use of individual presentation methods should be maintained throughout the Web site.

Content Types: Descriptions and Examples

Table 3–3 shows the content type, its description, and an example.

TABLE 3–3 Descriptions and Examples of Content Types

Type	Description	Example
Facts	Specific information in the form of a statement or data	IP Address for Allen's machine is 192.201.420.3
Concepts	Concepts and definitions are necessary for understanding what something is and what it is not.	What is a pencil? A **pencil** is a writing instrument that is handheld, cylindrical in shape, and contains graphite.
Procedures	Identify a sequential number of steps that tell you how to do something specific.	Adding Graphic: 1. Click on **Import Graphic**. 2. Select graphic from the menu. 3. Click the **OK** button.
Processes	Explain how something works. Involves flow of multiple events.	Phases of prototype development.
Principles	Principles and guidelines are general advice given by experts who have developed a knack for doing something well.	Avoid using frames.
Structures	Used for diagrams of objects that have parts and boundaries.	Circuit diagram. Parts of a computer command.

Example of Concept Content Type (Definitions)

Figure 3–2 is a page from the Human Factors Curriculum Web site[8] I developed while at Lucent Technologies. The page provides information on the common file extensions found on the Web. Notice how the label *Definition* is used. This usage provides consistency, and when people read this page, they have no doubt that definitions are being provided for the terms shown.

Example of Procedure Content Type (Step-by-Step Procedures)

Figure 3–3 is another page from my Human Factors Curriculum Web site[9] at Lucent Technologies. The page provides a procedure on viewing the results of customer transactions in Excel. Notice that the procedure is presented in a step-by-step manner. For consistency, all procedures in the Web site would be similarly formatted, i.e., have the same "look and feel." The reader's mind is patterned, and she expects to now see all procedures shown in the same way.

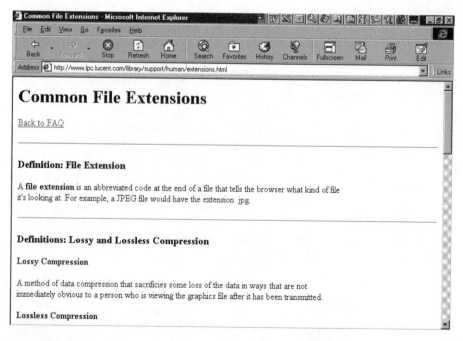

FIGURE 3–2 Human Factors Curriculum Web site. Concept content type.

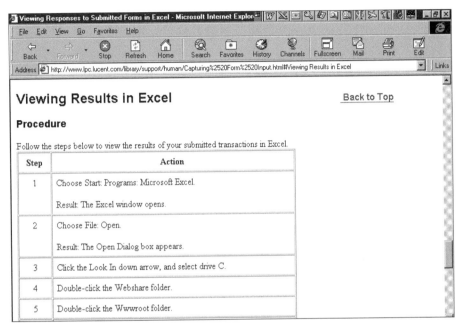

FIGURE 3-3 Human Factors Curriculum Web site. Procedure content type.

Representing Content Types on the Web

Table 3–4 shows recommendations for representing particular content types on the Web.

◆ Fundamental Principles Applied to Content

You will recall when we discussed navigation, we set forth four fundamental principles to apply in developing the navigation for a Web site. These same four principles can be applied to Web content, as shown in Table 3–5.

Assisting the User

The six content types covered above assist the user in learning about something or learning how to do something at your Web site. Users appreciate seeing this kind of content at a site because it is concrete, easy to follow, and encourages the user to take an action without having to resort to trial and error.

TABLE 3-4 Representing Content Types on the Web

Content type	Answers this question	Follow these guidelines
Facts	Which is which?	• Use tables to show codes, numbers, data, places, times, and so on.
Concepts	What is it?	• Write definitions consistently (see pencil example). • Take time to explain what the concept is not, e.g., the difference between pencils and pens. Pencils are not pens because they contain graphite not ink.* • Use graphics, JPEG images, photographs, etc., to show examples of concepts. • Use hyperlinks to render a pop-up definition of a term, which can be optionally selected.
Procedures	How do I do it?	• Number procedure steps and use action verb/object context. **Example: 1.** Type user name and press **ENTER.** • Each step should represent one logical reader action that can be held in short-term memory and performed.* • Tell the user the expected result for each step. • Embed small graphical features to help user. • Use links to show possible decisions or actions you might take.
Processes	How does it work?	• Separate processes into phases or stages. • Focus on movements, conditions, and their results. • Provide explanation of how the process works or what happens during the process. • Use graphics such as process flowcharts. • Use animation and video to dramatize how the process works. • **Caution:** Take a minimalist approach. Try animations rather than videos. Animations take up less resources and render faster. They may also exclude unnecessary detail and make the process easier to observe.

		• Audio may be useful for quick reviews of processes, but make sure audio is not different from what is on the screen. Do not have the user processing conflicting modalities of information, e.g., sound and animation.
Principles	What rules, guidelines, or policies exist? What would an expert do?	• Explain the cause and effect of the principle. • Identify the sources of the principle or policy. • Identify guidelines.
Structure	What does it look like?	• Show diagrams of circuits, switches. Elaborate with parts and functions highlighted on the diagram and detailed in a supporting table. • Show parts of computer commands. • Show parts of forms, e.g., invoices, employee vouchers. • Use in lieu of photographs and videos that show too much granularity and unnecessary detail. Can use animated graphics in lieu of videos and save on file size and storage.

(*Adapted from: Information Mapping, Inc. Internal Course Materials, 1999)

TABLE 3-5 Fundamental Principles Applied to Content

Principles	Applied to Web Content
Chunking	• Remember that people do not want to read, but prefer to scan on the Web. • Readers tend to look at information above the "fold" (bottom of the window expressed in newspaper terms). • Readers will spend about three or four seconds at your site to find something useful. • Chunking your information into four to six items makes it easier for readers to find and use information. • Use chunking at every level in your Web site so that the organization of your site is visible. • The reader then perceives your site as intuitive.
Relevance	• Put only relevant things together. • Irrelevancies confuse the reader and lower your credibility quickly.
Labeling	• Labeling information provides a quick way for your reader to access information. • Unlabeled chunks cause the reader to perform the non-value added work of conjuring up a label of her own, with the possible realization that you did not finish your work. • Labeling also helps you as a Web designer. • If you can't come up with a good label for a chunk of information, it's an indication that you have a mixed bag of stuff that needs to be pulled apart and either thrown out or put into another chunk(s). • Wordsmith a label so it is clear, precise, and descriptive of the nature of the information in your chunk. • Your label should be five words or less, with the emphasis on less. • Most of your labels should be around one to four words.
Consistency	• Consistent terminology and the consistent presentations and layout of information promote understanding. • If, for example, you have a term to define and decide to use the label *Definition,* stay with that label. Do not flip-flop to *What it's about* or some other synonym. • Your reader is looking, consciously or subconsciously, for patterns. • Any change in terminology should reflect the different nature of the information. • Again, no differences that do not make a difference.

◆ Prototyping

Introduction

A prototype is a model of a system. Prototypes can range on a continuum from low-fidelity (e.g., paper prototype) to high-fidelity (e.g., one using Java, XML, and Macromedia's Dreamweaver 3 and Flash 5). Low-fidelity prototypes are inexpensive, easy to build, and can often help to give the users an early idea of what the Web site will look like. Higher fidelity prototypes are more realistic but take longer to build.

Road to Success

Through prototyping, developers build a prototype, test the prototype, make design changes, test again, and continue this process until their prototype meets the reader's needs. Figure 3–4 shows the prototyping cycle.

Paper Prototyping

Before doing a high-fidelity prototype and investing a lot of time, it is often useful to build a paper prototype. Paper prototypes can be drawn on paper quickly, with radio buttons, check boxes, and other widgets sketched out. With a higher fidelity prototype, these widgets take longer to build and render on a page. With a paper prototype, early bad ideas can be ferreted out quickly and cheaply. The higher fidelity prototype can then be devoted to a design that is more likely to be closer to the user's expectations.

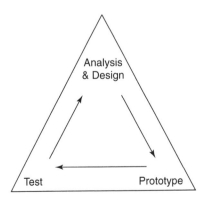

FIGURE 3-4 Prototyping cycle.

Paper prototypes are useful in inexpensively testing a conceptual model or metaphor of the site. If a desktop metaphor is shown to a nurse, he may not be able to relate the model to the job. On the other hand, if a nursing station metaphor is used, the nurse is likely to be better able to understand the proposed Web site and provide valuable feedback as to its potential efficacy.

Advantages of Prototyping

Prototyping enables us to get inside the minds of users and better manage their expectations. Concrete issues are more likely to emerge through use of a prototype than if abstract questions are asked. Some years back, the only available tools were flowcharts, data-flow diagrams, entity-relationship diagrams, and the like. These older tools portrayed only a static representation of the functionality of the system and did not address how the user would interact with the system and how the system might actually help the user. After many months of development, the typical user response at cutover was, "That's not what I wanted." Prototyping along with other complementary methodologies, such as event analysis, raise the likelihood of more quickly building systems and Web sites that meet users' needs.

Notes

1. Information Mapping, Inc., Internal Course Materials, 1999
2. Ibid
3. Ibid
4. Ibid
5. Ibid
6. Ibid
7. Ibid
8. Lucent Technologies, Learning and Performance Center, Internal Human Factors Web site, 1999
9. Ibid

4 Implementation and Testing

IN THIS CHAPTER

- Introduction

- Dreamweaver as an Implementation Tool

- Macromedia Dreamweaver 3

- Application: Shelley Biotechnologies

You have now designed your Web site's navigation and content. It is time to implement our design using a powerful software tool, Macromedia Dreamweaver 3. You'll learn enough about Dreamweaver 3 to confidently use this tool for any site that you are creating.

◆ Introduction

Implementing our Web site involves taking our design and writing the instructions necessary for the Web site to be physically built and published. Often this can involve a significant programming effort. However, with Dreamweaver 3 we can implement our site with a minimum of fuss and muss. We already have a thorough analysis and an efficient design. We may have even rough-sketched some of our potential Web pages on paper. Now we are ready for the physical implementation of our site, and then we will test our site to ensure that it meets users' needs.

◆ Before You Begin

Before you begin, let's go to the companion Web site that contains a logo image you will need to use in developing the Shelley Biotechnologies Web site using Dreamweaver 3. The Uniform Resource Locator (URL) is *http://www.phptr.com/essential*. The Web page you are taken to is entitled *Welcome to the Development Web Site!* When you get to the site, click on the hyperlink *Development Details*. You will then be taken to the *Development Details* Web page. The logo image is the first item on the page. Follow the instructions on the *Development Details* Web page to save the image, **logo.gif**, to your hard drive.

◆ Dreamweaver as an Implementation Tool

What is Macromedia Dreamweaver 3?

The following excerpt[1] best describes the nature of Macromedia Dreamweaver 3.

> Dreamweaver 3 is a professional visual editor for creating and managing Web sites and pages. With Dreamweaver 3, it's easy to create and edit cross-platform, cross-browser pages.
>
> Dreamweaver 3 provides advanced design and layout tools, as well as making it easy to use Dynamic HTML features such as animated layers and behaviors without writing a line of code. Browser-targeting checks your work for potential problems on all popular platforms and browsers. Macromedia's Roundtrip HTML technology imports HTML documents without formatting the code—and you can set Dreamweaver 3 to clean up and reformat HTML when you want to.
>
> Dreamweaver is fully customizable. You can create your own objects and commands, modify menus and keyboard shortcuts, and even write JavaScript code to extend Dreamweaver 3 with new behaviors and property inspectors.

Advantages of Dreamweaver

Dreamweaver 3 is one of the most respected and impressive software programs for Web design. Dreamweaver does not require any special software additions to the server to which the designed site is published. Dreamweaver produces HTML code with no browser-specific tags. I have used Dreamweaver in my classes on Web design and development. Students have found it intuitive to use and can get started with it very quickly. Dreamweaver works on both Windows and Macintosh systems.

Dreamweaver Tutorial

If you are new to Dreamweaver, you will want to go through the Dreamweaver Tutorial,[2] which is part of the Dreamweaver 3 software you purchased. For those experienced with Dreamweaver, the tutorial is optional.

After you complete the tutorial, you will be ready to apply Dreamweaver 3 to building the Shelley Biotechnologies, Inc. Web site.

◆ Using Dreamweaver to Implement the Shelley Biotechnologies Site

In Chapter 3, "Design," we developed a conceptual model, or metaphor, for Shelley Biotechnologies. We said that the site would contain graphics and diagrams in keeping with an engineering and scientific thinking process. Also in Chapter 3, we saw how we can then develop a navigation flowchart to lay out the architecture and navigation of the Shelley Biotechnologies site. In this chapter, we will use the navigation flowchart as the basis for developing a Site Map using Dreamweaver 3, which provides the capability of creating a Site Map right from the start. Then we can focus on our content, applying the ideas and principles covered in Chapter 3.

Throughout this chapter, I will be demonstrating for you, with step-by-step procedures, how we can build an effective Shelley Biotechnologies Web site. I recommend that you follow along and create the Shelley Biotechnologies site, using your own Macromedia Dreamweaver 3 software.

◆ Task Overview

Before we proceed, let's orient ourselves by looking at the tasks we will be performing in this chapter. They are shown in Table 4–1.

TABLE 4–1 Task Overview

Task No.	Task Description
1	Creating a Directory Folder
2	Launching Dreamweaver 3
3	Defining the Shelley Biotechnologies Web Site
4	Creating an index.htm Page
5	Creating a Product Folder and a Training Folder
6	Adding Additional Files to the Shelley Biotechnologies Web Site
7	Adding Minimal Content to the Shelley Biotechnologies Web Site
8	Creating a Site Map for Shelley Biotechnologies
9	Building the Shelley Biotechnologies Web Site
10	Completing the Shelley Biotechnologies Web Site

Task 1: Creating a Directory Folder

Follow these steps to create a directory folder.

1. Using your system's standard procedure to create a new directory folder on your hard drive.
2. Name the folder *Shelley*. This is the folder that will contain your created site and all of its elements.

Task 2: Launching Dreamweaver 3

Follow these steps to launch Dreamweaver 3.

1. Click on **Start** → **Program Files** → **Macromedia Dreamweaver 3**.

   Result: The Dreamweaver document window opens.

   Figure 4–1 shows the Dreamweaver document window.

Task 3: Defining the Shelley Biotechnologies Web Site

Follow these steps to define the Shelley Biotechnologies Web site.

1. On the document window menu bar click on **Site**, then **New Site**.

   Result: The dialog box entitled Site Definition for Unnamed Site 2 appears.

   Figure 4–2 shows the Site Definition for Unnamed Site 2 dialog box.

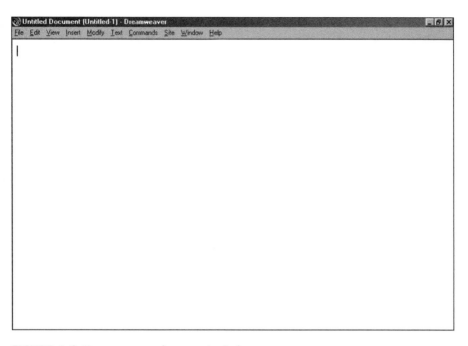

FIGURE 4–1 Dreamweaver document window.

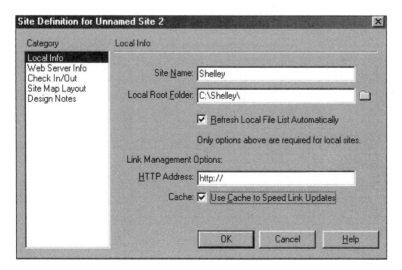

FIGURE 4–2 Site Definition for Unnamed Site 2 dialog box.

2. Type *Shelley* in the Site Name text box.
3. Make sure that the **Refresh Local File List Automatically** check box is selected.
4. Click the **Browse** button to navigate to and select the Shelley folder you created in Task 1: Creating a Directory Folder. The **Browse** button is the folder icon to the right of the Local Root Folder text box.
5. Click the **OK** button in the Site Definition for Unnamed Site 1 dialog box.

   Result: A dialog box appears asking if you want to create a cache file, as shown in Figure 4–3.

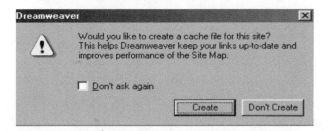

FIGURE 4–3 Dialog box offers the option to create a cache file.

6. Click the **Don't Create** button.

   Result: The Define Sites dialog box appears, as shown in Figure 4–4.

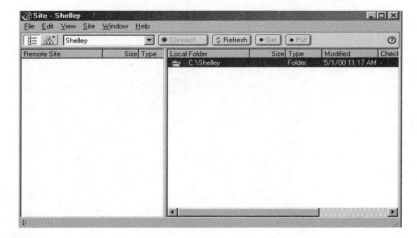

FIGURE 4–4 The Define Sites dialog box.

Task 4: Creating an index.htm Page

Follow these steps to create an index.htm file for Shelley Biotechnologies.

1. On the Site window menu bar, Click on **File→ New File.**
   Result: A file called **untitled.htm** appears in the right panel of the Site window under the Shelley folder.
   Figure 4–5 shows the **untitled.htm** file highlighted in the right panel.

FIGURE 4–5 The **untitled.htm** file is highlighted in the right panel.

2. Type *index.htm* to rename the untitled.htm file and press **Enter**.
   Result: The untitled.htm file is renamed **index.htm**, as shown in Figure 4–6.

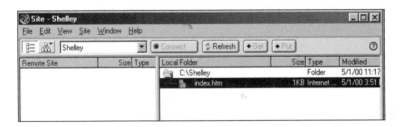

FIGURE 4–6 The renamed file, **index.htm,** is highlighted in the right panel.

◆ Creating the Remaining Files for Shelley Biotechnologies

Background

Before we create a Site Map for Shelley Biotechnologies, it is easier if we create skeleton pages representing the files in the Web site. We will create files for the following Web pages:

1. Product Pages
   a. Portable BioLab
   b. Portable BioLab Access
   c. Educational Products
   d. Corporate BioLabs
   e. Enterprise BioLabs
   f. How to Order Products
2. Training Pages
   a. Genetic Engineering for Beginners
   b. Intermediate Genetic Engineering
   c. Advanced Genetic Engineering
   d. Professor Track Biogenesis
   e. rDNA Refresher Course
   f. Build Your Training Schedule

We will create two folders within the Shelley Biotechnologies site to contain these files: a Products folder and a Training folder. Then we will create individual skeletal files, which will be the individual Web pages within each of these two folders.

Task 5: Creating a Products Folder and a Training Folder

Follow these steps to create a Products folder and a Training folder for Shelley Biotechnologies.

1. On the right panel of the Site window, highlight the root directory folder C:\Shelley.

   Figure 4–7 shows the C:\Shelley root directory folder highlighted.

FIGURE 4–7 The C:\Shelly root directory folder is highlighted.

2. On the **menu bar** of the Site window, select **File→New Folder**.

   Result: A new folder called **untitled** appears in the right panel of the Site window, as shown in Figure 4–8.

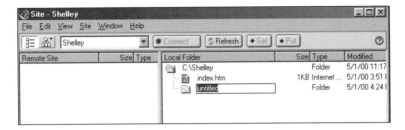

FIGURE 4–8 The new folder, **untitled,** appears in the right panel.

3. Rename the untitled folder *Products* and press **Enter.**

Result: The untitled folder is renamed **Products.**
Figure 4–9 shows the Products folder under C:\Shelley.

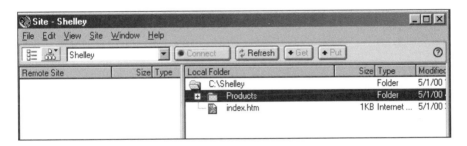

FIGURE 4–9 The Products folder under C:\Shelley.

4. Repeat steps 2 and 3 to create a Training folder under
C:\Shelley.

Hint: Be sure the root directory C:\Shelley is highlighted before creating the Training folder.

Result: There should now be two folders under the root
directory C:\Shelley, the Products folder and the Training folder, and the right panel of your Site window
should be the same as that shown in Figure 4–10.

Task 6: Adding Additional Files to the Shelley Biotechnologies Web Site

In Task 6 we will be adding additional files to the Shelley
Biotechnologies site. We will save some of the files in the Products
folder and others in the Training folder.

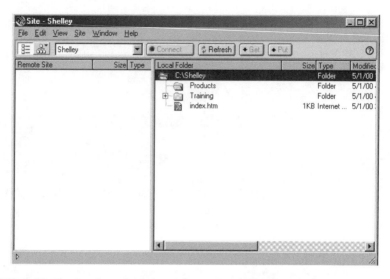

FIGURE 4–10 The Products folder and the Training folder under `C:\Shelley`.

The files we create will have only a Heading 1, identifying the name of the page. We will also add a title to the page, which will be the same as the Heading 1. For example, for the Products Web page, we will create a file called products.htm. The Heading 1 on the page will read Products. We will use Page Properties to change the title of the page, which appears in the title bar of the Products page.

In effect, we are creating pages with practically no content except for the Heading 1 and the title of the page. I find this to be a great way to prepare to set up a Site Map. On the home page, we will create two text hyperlinks: one to the Products page and one to the Training page. Then, on the Products page, we will create text hyperlinks to each of the six individual Products pages. And finally, on the Training page, we will create text hyperlinks to each of the individual Training pages.

In this way, we will have laid out the structure of our site in the Site Map. We will be able to choose to view the Site Map showing the titles of the Web pages or showing the filenames of the Web pages.

In Task 7, we will be adding minimal content to the Shelley Biotechnologies Web site.

In Task 8, we will actually create a Site Map for the site.

Follow these steps to add the additional files to the Shelley Biotechnologies site.

1. Press **F5** to open the Site window and highlight the Products folder.

   Result: The Site window appears with the Products folder highlighted, as shown in Figure 4-11.

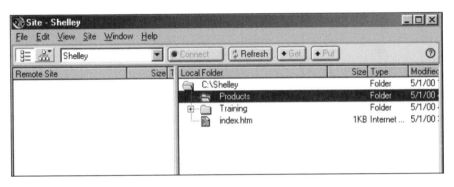

FIGURE 4–11 The Products folder is highlighted in the Site window.

2. On the Site window menu bar, select **File→New File.**

   Result: A new file called **untitled** appears in high-lighted mode in the right panel of the Site window under the Products folder.

3. Rename the untitled file to **products.htm** and press **Enter**.

   Result: The untitled file is renamed to **products.htm.** Figure 4–12 shows the results of steps 1, 2, and 3.

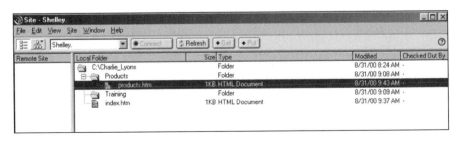

FIGURE 4–12 The Site window shows the results of steps 1, 2, and 3.

4. Repeat step 2 to put the remaining files into the Products folder.

The remaining files are

- **portable_biolab.htm**
- **portable_biolab_access.htm**
- **educational_products.htm**
- **corporate_biolabs.htm**
- **enterprise_biolabs.htm**
- **how_to_order.htm**

Result: All of the product files are now in the Products folder. Your Site window should look like the window in Figure 4–13.

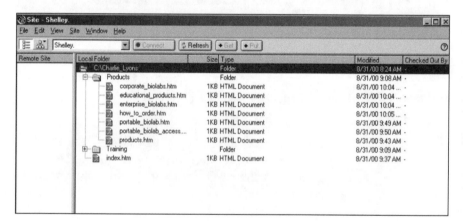

FIGURE 4–13 The Products folder contains all of the product files.

5. Repeat step 2 to add the following files to the Training folder.

The files to be added to the Training folder are:

- **training.htm**
- **genetic_eng_beginners.htm**
- **intermediate_genetic_eng.htm**
- **advanced_genetic_eng.htm**
- **professor_track_biogenesis.htm**
- **rdna_refresher_course.htm**
- **build_your_training_sched.htm**

Result: The above files are added to the Training folder.

Figure 4–14 shows the Products and Training folders and the files added to each.

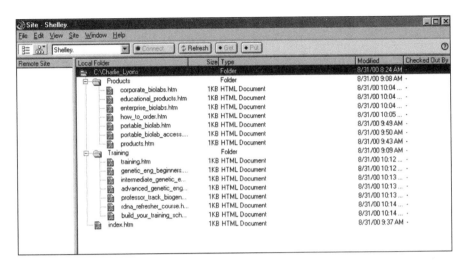

FIGURE 4–14 The files have been added to the Products and Training folders.

Task 7: Adding Minimal Content to the Shelley Biotechnologies Web Site

Now that we have created our files for Shelley Biotechnologies, we can build our Site Map. In Dreamweaver, our Site Map will show the organization of the site as well as both physical and relative links.

In Task 7, we are going to add some minimal content to the pages created above. This minimal content will consist of a Heading 1 and a Page Title. On the home page, the Products page, and the Training page, we will also add text hyperlinks to each of the subpages below the Products and Training pages.

Follow these steps to add minimal content to created pages.

1. Press **F5** to open the Site window.
2. Double click on the **index.htm** file.

   Result: The index.htm file opens in the document window.

3. Make sure your mouse pointer is at the top left of the window and select **Heading 1** from the Property Inspector.
4. Type *Welcome to Shelley Biotechnologies!* and press **Enter** twice.

   Result: Welcome to Shelley Biotechnologies! appears as a Heading 1 on the top left of the page.

5. Move your mouse pointer to anywhere on the page.
6. Click the right-mouse button.

   Result: A pop-up menu appears near where you clicked.

7. Select **Page Properties,** which is the last menu item on the pop-up menu.

   Result: The Page Properties dialog box appears.

8. In the Page Properties text box, type *Welcome to Shelley Biotechnologies!* and click the **OK** button.

   Result: The Page Properties dialog box closes and Welcome to Shelley Biotechnologies! appears in the title bar at the top of the document window.

   Figure 4–15 shows how your document window should look now.

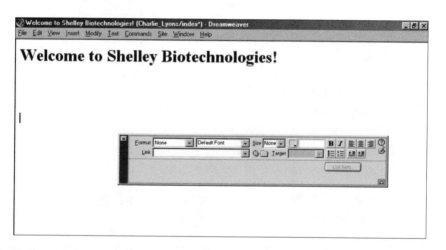

FIGURE 4–15 Welcome to Shelley Biotechnologies! appears in the title bar.

9. In the Properties Inspector, change the **Format** to **None.**
10. Type *Products* and highlight it.
11. On the Properties Inspector, click on the folder icon to the right of the Link text box.

    Result: The Select File dialog box appears.

12. Make sure that the Products folder appears in the Look in: text box.
13. Select the **products** file and click the **Select** button.

    Result: The hyperlink is established from the Welcome to Shelley Biotechnologies home page to the Products page.

14. Click outside the text hyperlink and move to another line.

15. Type *Training* and highlight it.

16. Repeat steps 11 through 14 to set up a link on the Welcome to Shelley Biotechnologies! home page to the Training page.

Result: Your Welcome to Shelley Biotechnologies! home page should now be linked to the Products page and the Training page.

Figure 4–16 shows how your document window should now look.

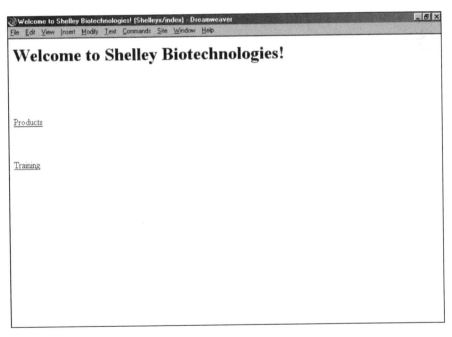

FIGURE 4–16 The home page contains hyperlinks to the Products and Training pages.

17. Press **F5** to open the Site window.

18. Double-click on the **products.htm** file in the Products folder.

Result: The products.htm file opens in the document window.

19. Add *Shelley Biotechnologies' Products* to the title bar and as a Heading 1 on the Products page.

20. Type in the titles of each of the six product files and establish a hyperlink for each from the Products page to each of these six individual Product pages.

HINT:
You can find the names of the Products pages on the Shelley Site View.

Result: The Products page is hyperlinked to each of the six individual Product pages, as shown in Figure 4–17.

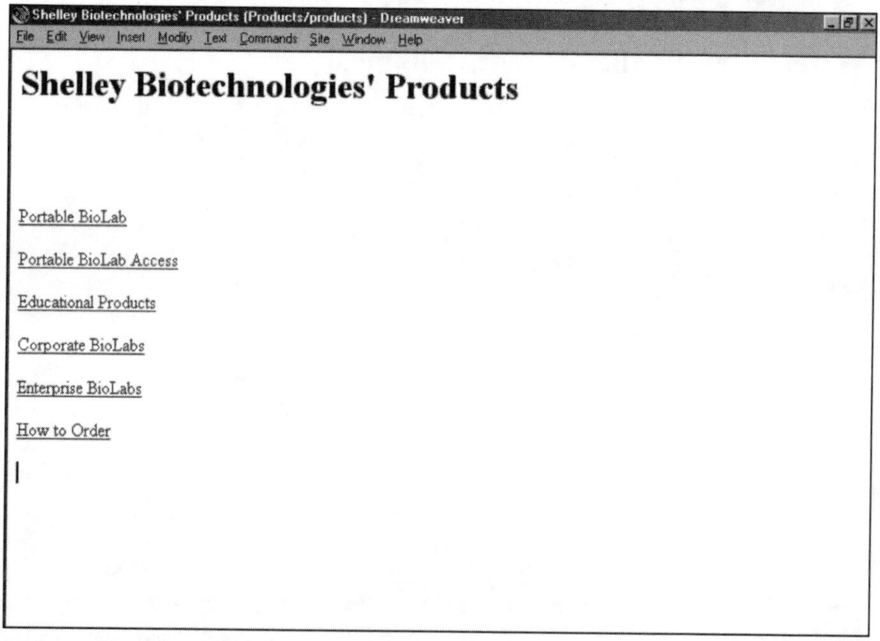

FIGURE 4–17 The Products page contains hyperlinks for each individual Product page.

21. Add *Shelley Biotechnologies' Training* to the title bar and as a Heading 1 on the Training page.

22. Type in the titles of each of the six training files and establish hyperlinks from the Training page to each of these six individual Training pages.

Figure 4–18 shows how your Training page should look with the hyperlinks to the Training pages.

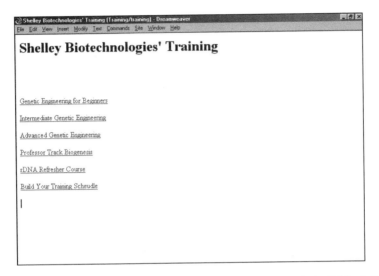

FIGURE 4–18 The Training Page contains hyperlinks to each individual Training page.

Task 8: Creating the Site Map for Shelley Biotechnologies

In Chapter 3, "Design," we built a navigation flowchart showing the architecture and navigation for our Shelley Biotechnologies site. As we said earlier, we may have even paper-prototyped a few pages. In this chapter, we have so far created a skeletal framework of the site and have actually set down our navigation as we see it so far. Creating the Site Map is easy. We've got the ingredients.

Before we create the Shelley Biotechnologies Site Map, we need to add headings and page titles to the Product and Training pages. It is particularly important to have our page titles since we may wish to use these rather than filenames in our Site Map.

Follow these steps to add Headings and Page Titles to the Product and Training pages

1. Applying what you have learned so far, proceed to add Heading 1s and page titles to each of the Product and Training pages.
2. Proceed to the next procedure, Creating the Shelley Biotechnologies Site Map.

Follow these steps to create the Shelley Biotechnologies Site Map.

1. Press **F5** to open the Site window for Shelley Biotechnologies. Figure 4–19 shows how your Site window should look.

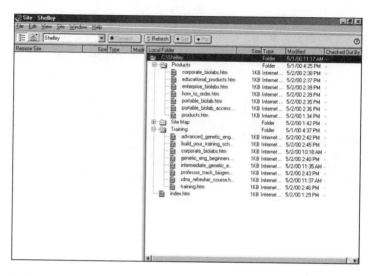

FIGURE 4–19 Shelley Biotechnologies Site window.

2. Click on the **Site Map** button in the upper left corner of the Site window.

The Site Map button is highlighted in the left panel of the Site window in Figure 4–20.

Figure 4–21 shows how your Site window should now look. Notice that the Site Map shows filenames.

3. On the menu bar, click on the **View**, then **Show Page Titles**.

Result: Your Site Map now shows page titles, which tend to be more descriptive.

Figure 4–22 shows how your Site Map should look using page titles.

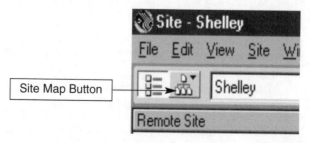

FIGURE 4–20 The Site Map button is in the upper left corner of the Site window.

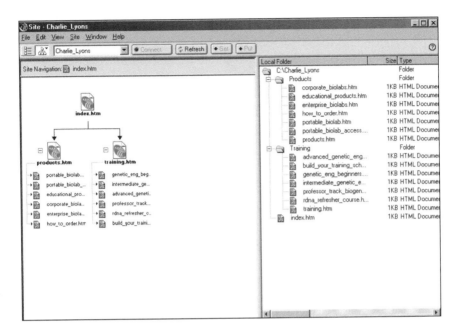

FIGURE 4–21 The Site window contains a Site Map in the left panel.

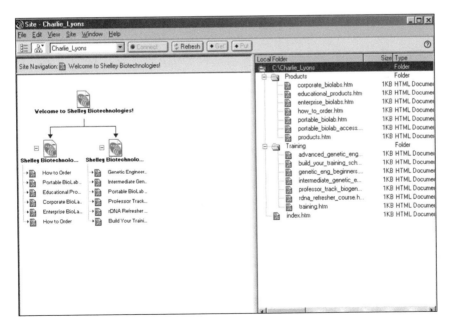

FIGURE 4–22 The Site Map with page titles instead of filenames.

◆ Where We Are

So far, we have created a skeleton version of our Shelley Biotechnologies Web site. That is, we have all the Web pages created with minimal content. We have also established our linkage and created a Site Map to guide us. On the Site Map, we have chosen to show the Web page titles as opposed to the filenames. You can, however, use either page titles or filenames on your Site Map. Since the page titles are more expressive, it makes it easier to read the Site Map from a human factors perspective.

Our Next Step

Our next step is to develop the content for each of the Web pages and complete our Shelley Biotechnologies Web site design. As we do this, we may make changes to our Site Map. We may also add Web pages, delete Web pages, and even combine Web pages. Our goal is to come up with the most efficacious site from human factors, usability, and engineering perspectives.

You will be accessing certain files and graphics from a companion Web site *http://www.phptr.com/essential,* and importing them into your design. You will start with the home page and continue through each of the other pages, adding content from your specification as it is developed so far, as well as from the Web site.

Task 9: Building the Shelley Biotechnologies Web Site

Follow these steps to build the Shelley Biotechnologies home page content.

1. Open Dreamweaver 3 and press **F5** to open the Site window.
2. In the right panel of the Site window, double-click on the **index.htm** file.

   Result: The index.htm file (Welcome to Shelley Technologies! home page as you originally created it) opens in the document window, as shown in Figure 4–23.
3. Place your mouse pointer anywhere on the **Welcome to Shelley Biotechnologies!** home page and right-click.

   Result: A pop-up menu appears.
4. On the pop-up menu, select **Page Properties**.

   Result: The Page Properties dialog box appears, as shown in Figure 4–24.

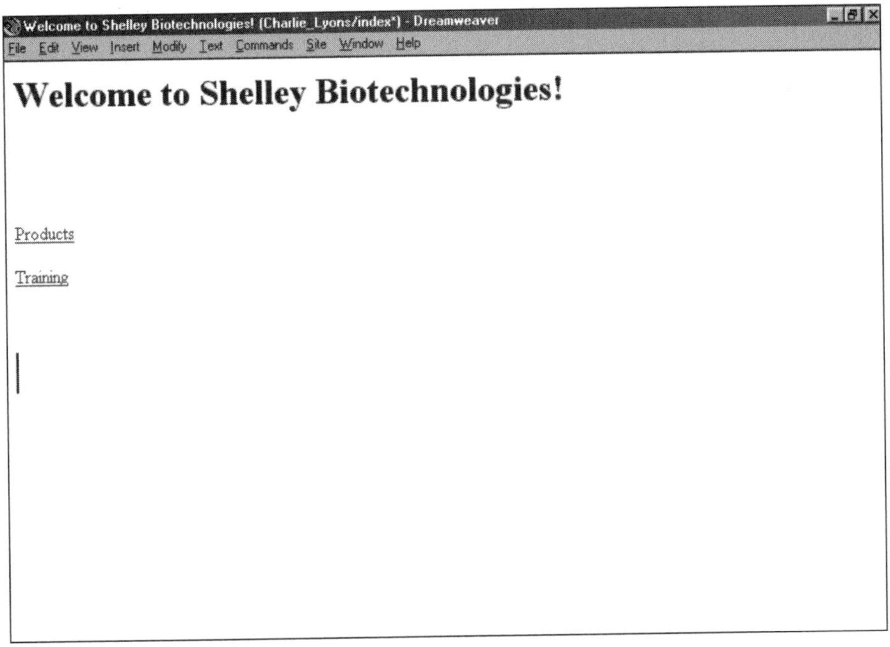

FIGURE 4–23 The Welcome to Shelley Biotechnologies! home page.

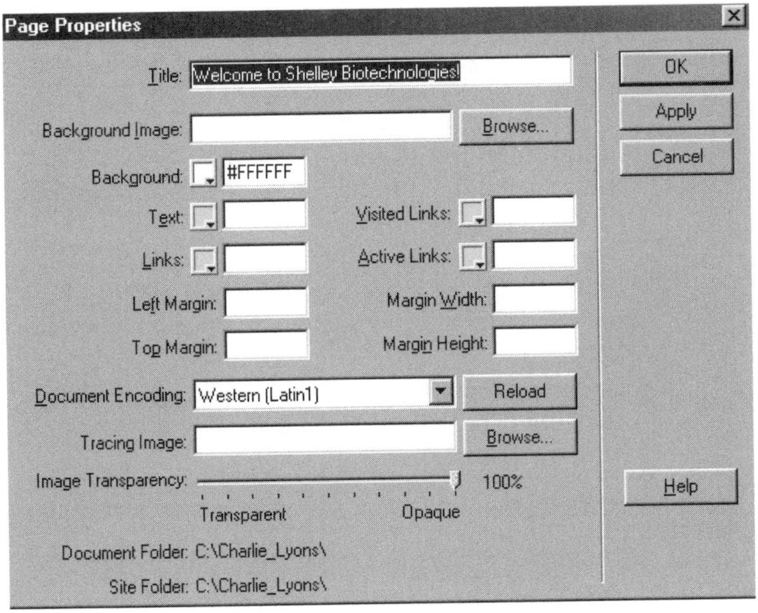

FIGURE 4–24 Page Properties dialog box.

5. Click on the small down-arrow next to **Background** to change the background color of the home page.

Result: The Color Palette will appear, as shown in Figure 4–25.

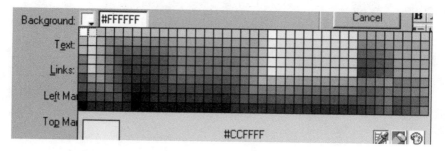

FIGURE 4–25 The Color Palette.

6. Select the **color** in the first row, second column, and left-click on your mouse.

Result: The Color Palette closes and the background page changes to a light blue.

NOTE:

The hexadecimal equivalent of the color you have chosen appears in the Page Properties dialog box to the right of the background color selected.

7. Place your mouse pointer to the left of the Welcome to Shelley Biotechnologies Heading 1 and press **Enter** twice.

8. Place your mouse pointer at the top left of the page above the **Welcome to Shelley Biotechnologies!** home page Heading 1.

9. On the menu bar, select **Insert,** then **Table**.

Result: The Insert Table dialog box appears, shown in Figure 4–26.

10. Select **one row, two columns,** a width of **100 percent,** and make the border 1. The table you have inserted is shown in Figure 4–27.

NOTE:

Make sure the table borders show. This makes the table more visible during design. When we are done, you can make the table border **0,** and it will not be visible to the Web page reader.

11. Place your mouse pointer in the left cell of the table you just inserted and change the Format to **Heading 1**, using the Properties Inspector.

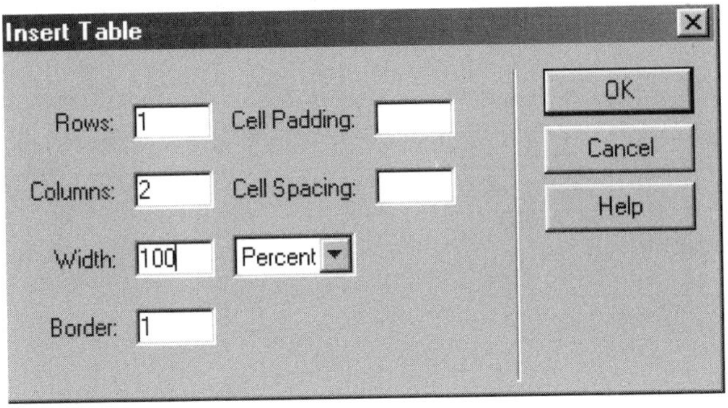

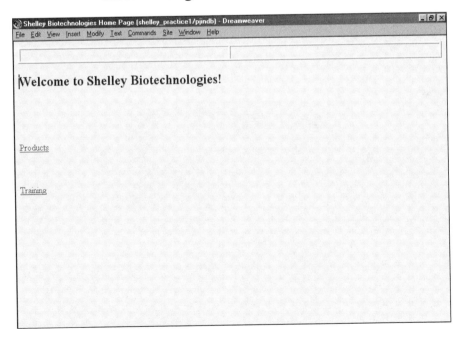

FIGURE 4–26 The Insert Table dialog box.

12. Cut and paste the Heading 1 you previously created into the left cell of the table, as shown in Figure 4–28.

13. Select the Heading 1 text called **Welcome to Shelley Biotechnologies!**

FIGURE 4–27 The table appears above the Heading 1.

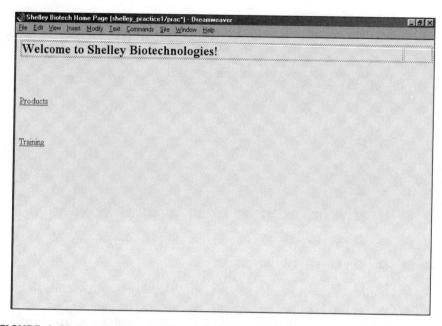

FIGURE 4–28 Heading 1, Welcome to Shelley Biotechnologies!, is in the left cell of the table.

14. On the menu bar, select **Text,** then **CSS Styles,** then **Edit Style Sheet.**

Result: The Edit Style Sheet dialog box appears, as shown in Figure 4–29.

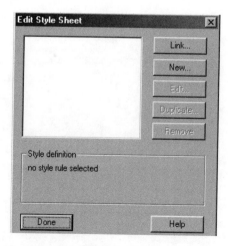

FIGURE 4–29 The Edit Style Sheet dialog box.

15. Click on the **New** button.

Result: The New Style dialog box appears, as shown in Figure 4–30.

FIGURE 4–30 The New Style dialog box.

16. Select the second radio button, **Redefine HTML Tag**.

Result: The h1 tag should appear in the Tag drop-down box.

17. Click the **OK** button.

Result: A dialog box called Style definition for h1 appears, as show in Figure 4–31.

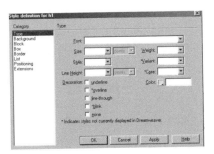

FIGURE 4–31 Style definition for h1 dialog box.

18. Be sure that **Type** is selected in the Category window on the left.

19. Use the table below to enter the required attribute values into the Style definition for h1.

TABLE 4–2 Required Attribute Values

Attribute	Value
Font	Helvetica, sans serif
Size	24 points
Weight	Bold
Style	Italic

20. Click the OK button after entering the above values for each of the attributes.

Result: The Edit Style Sheet dialog box appears with h1 highlighted, as shown in Figure 4–32.

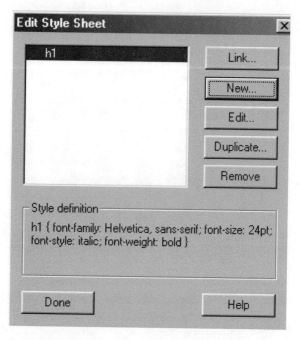

FIGURE 4–32 The Edit Style Sheet with h1 highlighted.

21. Click the Done button.

Figure 4–33 shows how your Welcome to Shelley Biotechnologies! home page should look.

FIGURE 4–33 The home page with h1 style definitions applied.

22. On the Welcome to Shelley Biotechnologies! home page, left-click in the right cell next to the Heading 1 called Welcome to Shelley Biotechnologies!

23. If you have not done so already, copy the **logo.gif** file from your desktop to the C:\Shelley folder.

24. On the menu bar, click on **Insert,** then **Image.**

Result: The Select Image Source dialog box appears, shown in Figure 4–34.

25. Make sure that the Shelley folder appears in the Look in drop down menu.

26. Double-click on the **logo** image file.

Result: The logo image is inserted into the right cell of the table, as shown in Figure 4–35.

27. Adjust the table borders so that the office image fits appropriately next to the Heading 1.

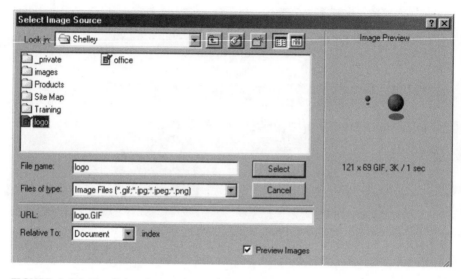

FIGURE 4–34 The Select Image Source dialog box.

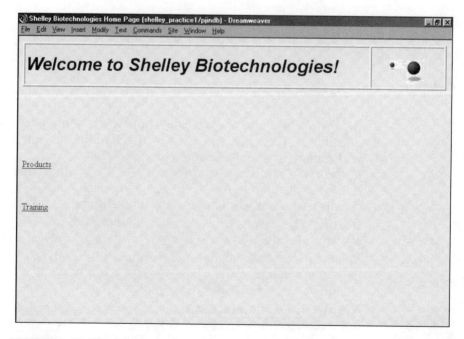

FIGURE 4–35 The Welcome to Shelley Biotechnologies! home page with the logo image inserted.

◆ Completing the Welcome to Shelley Biotechnologies! Home Page

You are going to be provided with the information to complete the Welcome to Shelley Biotechnologies! home page. Before we do that, though, let's take a look at the final home page product so you have an idea of what your page will look like. Figure 4–36 shows the finished Welcome to Shelley Biotechnologies! home page. You can also see a color view of this page at *http://www.phptr.com/essential*.

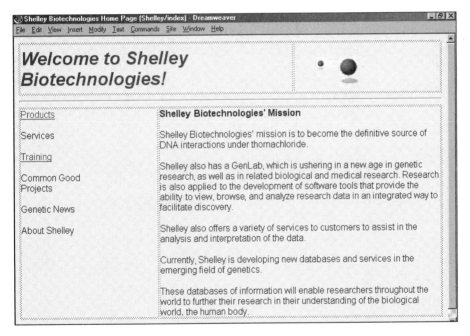

FIGURE 4–36 The finished Welcome to Shelley Biotechnologies! home page.

Follow these steps to enter the remaining information on your Welcome to Shelley Biotechnologies! home page.

1. Make sure you have inserted a horizontal rule under your Heading 1.
2. Insert a two-column, one-row table with the attributes shown in Figure 4–37.

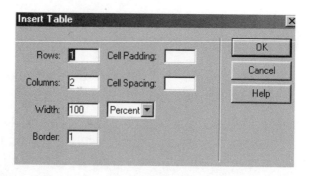

FIGURE 4–37 Attribute settings for a two-column, one-row table.

3. Cut and paste into the left column of the table the Products and Training text hyperlinks that you inserted earlier.
4. Put your mouse pointer to the right of Products and press **Enter**.
5. Type the word *Services*.

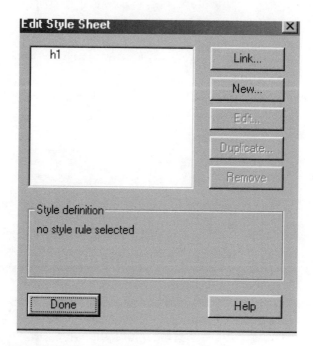

FIGURE 4–38 The Edit Style dialog box.

6. Put your mouse pointer to the right of the Training text hyperlink and press **Enter**.
7. Repeat steps 4 and 5 to add
   - *Common Good Projects*
   - *Genetic News*
   - *About Shelley*
8. Save what you have done so far.
9. Select all of the text you have just entered in the left column of the table.
10. On the menu bar, select **Text→CSS Styles→Edit Style Sheets**.

    Result: The Edit Style dialog box appears, as shown in Figure 4–38.
11. Click on the **New** button.

    Result: The New Style dialog box appears, as shown in Figure 4–39.

FIGURE 4–39 The New Style dialog box.

12. Select the **Redefine HTML Tag**.
13. In the Tag drop-down menu, select **td** and click the **OK** button.

    Result: The Style definition for td dialog box appears, as shown in Figure 4–40.
14. In the Category panel (left panel), make sure **Type** is selected.
15. Select the following attributes for font and size, leaving the other attributes with the default values.

    Font: **Helvetica, sans-serif**
    Size: **12 points**

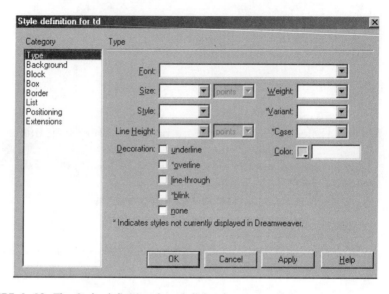

FIGURE 4–40 The Style definition for td dialog box.

> **16.** Click the **OK** button in the Style definition for td dialog box.
>
> **Result:** The Style definition for td dialog box closes, revealing the Edit Style Sheet dialog box, as shown in Figure 4–41.

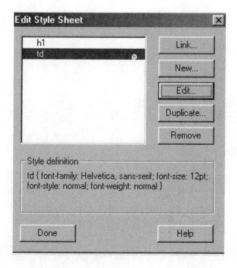

FIGURE 4–41 The Edit Style Sheet dialog box.

17. Click the **Done** button.

Result: The Edit Style Sheet dialog box closes, revealing your Welcome to Shelley Biotechnologies! home page, as modified so far.

18. Check to see that your page looks like the one shown in Figure 4–42.

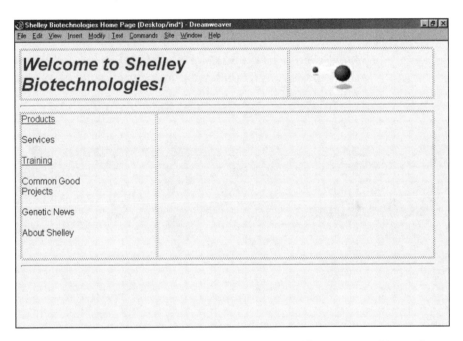

FIGURE 4–42 The Welcome to Shelley Biotechnologies! home page with text hyperlinks set in a table.

INSERTING SHELLEY BIOTECHNOLOGIES' MISSION STATEMENT

So far, you have modified the skeletal home page to include a Heading 1 with an image and the navigation links shown on the left of the home page. You have used tables as a way to line up your work so that it will render appropriately in various browsers. You have kept your design simple, but have used CSS Style Sheets to tailor your Heading 1 and your text link fonts.

Next, you will insert Shelley Biotechnologies' Mission Statement into the right column of the table containing your text hyperlinks. When you are finished, you will remove the table borders so that a reader of the page is not aware that you chose tables to line up your work. When you finish inserting the Shelley Biotechnologies Mission Statement, you will add a simple horizontal rule below the invisible table to help group your page into chunks. As you know, this makes it easier for readers to scan the page and find what they need.

Follow these steps to insert the Shelley Biotechnologies Mission Statement into the Welcome to Shelley Biotechnologies! home page.

1. Make sure that the Welcome to Shelley Biotechnologies! home page is open and active in your Dreamweaver document window.
2. If you need to, resize the table so that it looks like Figure 4–43.

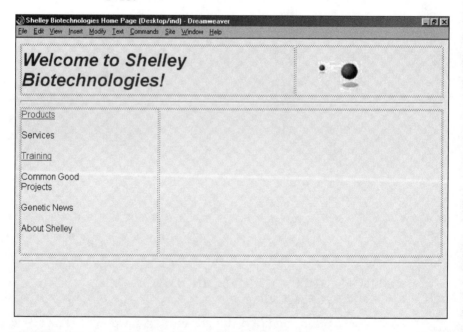

FIGURE 4–43 The Welcome to Shelley Biotechnologies! home page as it should now look.

3. Follow the table below.

If you wish to	Then
Type in the Shelley Biotechnologies Mission	Go to step 4.
Insert the Shelley Biotechnologies Mission from the Companion Web site	Go to step 6.

4. Type the following text into the right column of the table you created:

Shelley Biotechnologies' Mission
    Shelley Biotechnologies' mission is to become the definitive source of DNA interactions under thornachloride.
    Shelley also has a GenLab, which is ushering in a new age in genetic research, as well as in related biological and medical research. Research is also applied to the development of software tools that provide the ability to view, browse, and analyze research data in an integrated way to facilitate discovery.
    Shelley also offers a variety of services to customers to assist in the analysis and interpretation of the data.
    Currently, Shelley is developing new databases and services in the emerging field of genetics.
    These databases of information will enable researchers throughout the world to further their research in their understanding of the biological world.

5. Go to step 8.
6. Access the Companion Web site *(http://www.phptr.com/ essential)* and copy the Shelley Biotechnologies Mission to your clipboard.
7. Insert the Shelley Biotechnologies Mission in the right column of the table.
8. Select the entire text of Shelley Biotechnologies' Mission.
9. On the menu bar, select **Text→CSS Style Sheet→Edit Style Sheet**.
10. On the Edit Style Sheet dialog box, select **New**, then **td**.
    Result: The Style definition for td appears, as shown in Figure 4–44.
11. For the Font, select **Helvetica, sans serif.**
12. For Size, select **12 point**.
13. Click the **OK** button.
    Result: The Style definition for td dialog box closes revealing your home page.
14. Select the text Shelley Biotechnologies' Mission.
15. In the Properties Inspector, select **bold.**
    Result: The text heading Shelley Biotechnologies' Mission appears in bold and the remainder of the text appears in normal font.
16. Click to the right of the bottom of the table and press **Enter**.

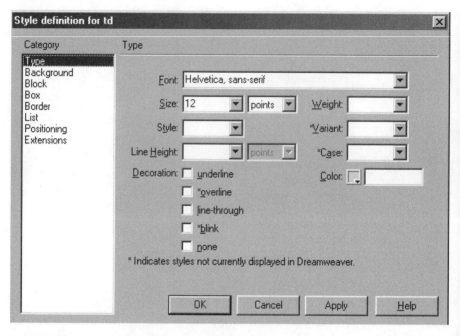

FIGURE 4–44 The Style definition for td dialog box.

17. On the menu bar, select **Insert→Horizontal Rule**.

Result: A horizontal rule appears under the table containing your hyperlinks and Shelley Biotechnologies' Mission.

18. Make any final spacing adjustments.

19. For all of the tables on the home page, change the border size to **0** so that your reader will not be able to discern that you used tables to line up your work.

20. Check your work against Figure 4–45 and against the Shelley site, *http://www.phptr.com/essential,* making any final adjustments.

21. Press **F12** to view your Welcome to Shelley Biotechnologies! home page in your browser and make any final adjustments in your Dreamweaver document window.

Figure 4–46 shows how your Welcome to Shelley Biotechnologies! home page should now look in your browser.

22. Check your work once again comparing it to the browser version on the Shelley Web site *http://www.phptr.com/essential.*

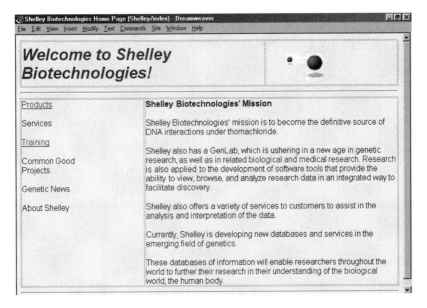

FIGURE 4-45 The Welcome to Shelley Biotechnologies! home page now contains the Shelley Biotechnologies' mission.

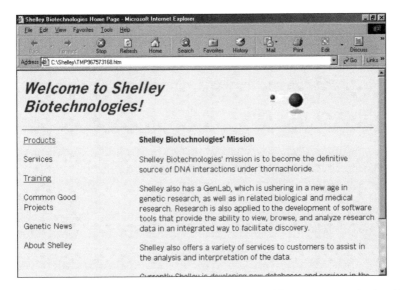

FIGURE 4-46 The Welcome to Shelley Biotechnologies! home page as it should appear in your browser.

Task 10: Completing the Shelley Biotechnologies Web Site

So far, you have done the following:

- Created a Shelley Biotechnologies skeletal Web site to include a Site Map
- Completed the Welcome to Shelley Biotechnologies! home page.

Next, we will go through creating the Product Web page. If you remember, for the Welcome to Shelley Biotechnologies! home page, we showed our navigation on the left side of the page. These text hyperlinks are links to pages that are at a lower level in our Site Map. However, now we will be creating pages that will link to pages at a lower level as well as to those at the same level. The links to pages at the same hierarchical level will be placed horizontally across the top of the Web page under the Heading 1 and its associated image.

Now we have established a standard, namely, links to child pages shown vertically on the left and links to pages at the same level shown horizontally at the top.

So far, to support you in developing your Welcome to Shelley Biotechnologies! home page using Dreamweaver 3, we took a detailed step-by-step approach. Now that you are used to using Dreamweaver and have completed the Welcome to Shelley Biotechnologies! home page, we will show you new distinctions that you may not have used before with Dreamweaver.

1. Setting up the horizontal navigation for pages at the same level.
2. Creating forms.

For setting up the horizontal navigation for pages at the same level, we will use the Product page as an example. However, once we have demonstrated the use of the horizontal text hyperlinks for pages at the same level, we will leave it to you to finish the remainder of the page on your own. We will show you an example of how your page should look, so that you can check your work when you are done.

For creating forms, we will take you through the creation of one form, How to Order, and leave it to you to finish the other form, Build Your Training Schedule. Again, we will provide final examples of the completed pages so you can check your work.

RECOMMENDATION:
Please take the time to complete the design of the entire site. The very act of creating the pages and seeing how everything ties together provides insights that cannot be gotten simply by looking at the final suggested solution.

Simply put, the best way to learn design and Dreamweaver 3 is by *doing*. But then, you know that.

◆ Completing the Products Web Page

Follow these steps to complete the Products Web page.

1. Open Dreamweaver 3 and bring the Products Web page up in the document window.

HINT:
Remember, the Products Web page is in the Products folder.

Figure 4–47 shows the Products Web page.

2. Using the Welcome to Shelley Biotechnologies! home page you have already created as a model, perform steps 3 through 5.

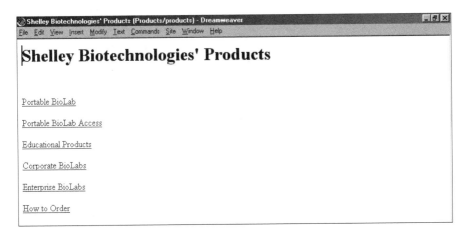

FIGURE 4–47 The Shelley Biotechnologies' Products Web page.

3. Move the Heading 1 into a table and modify the Heading 1 according to the style used for your Welcome to Shelley Biotechnologies! home page.
4. Insert the **logo.gif** image in the appropriate place in the table, adjusting its size accordingly.
5. Insert a horizontal rule under the Heading 1 and the **logo.gif** image.

INSERTING THE HORIZONTAL NAVIGATION HYPERTEXT LINKS

REMINDER:
Earlier, we referred to inserting the horizontal navigation hypertext links and said that these were for navigation to and from pages at the same level.

Follow these steps to insert the horizontal navigation hypertext links.

1. Place your mouse pointer below the horizontal rule on the Products Web page.
2. Insert a table of one row and seven columns at 100 percent width.

NOTE:
At this point, you can decide whether or not you want to have your borders on while working in the document window.

3. Type the following text hyperlinks in each column of the table, starting from the left:
   • *Home*
   • *Products*
   • *Services*
   • *Training*
   • *Common Good Projects*
   • *Genetic News*
   • *About Shelley*
4. Using CSS Style Sheets, change the appearance of these text items as follows:
   Text: Helvetica, sans serif
   Font: 12 points
5. Change the Products text to red color, italic.

6. For the remaining six text items, create hyperlinks to the appropriate files.
7. Create vertical child hyperlinks on the left side.

HINT:
Remember to create a table to line up your work and to use your Site Map to determine your child navigation.

8. Type the following text regarding Shelley Biotechnologies' Products and modify it appropriately, using the CSS Style Sheet.

NOTE:
You can download the text from the Companion Web site, *(http://www.phptr.com/essential)*, and insert it if you prefer.

Shelley Biotechnologies' Products
Shelley Biotechnologies is proud of its array of products. There is a Portable BioLab, which can be transported to a client's location to conduct onsite analysis. Shelley can also provide access to clients to visit a location and have direct access to the Portable BioLab.
Shelley Biotechnologies is proud of its educational products and is confident your expectations will be met and exceeded with our motto of *building quality in from the beginning.*
The company encourages you to find out how to order its products. It provides shocking levels of responsiveness in meeting its customers' needs.

9. Insert a horizontal rule under the text hyperlinks and the text regarding Shelley Biotechnologies' Products.
10. Compare your product to the example shown in Figure 4–49 and make any adjustments.

NOTE:
You may also compare your product to the example shown on the companion Web site *(http://www.phptr.com/essential)*.

Figure 4–48 shows the completed Shelley Biotechnologies' Products Web page.
11. View your page in your browser and test all of your hyperlinks.
Figure 4–49 shows an example of Shelley Biotechnologies' Products Web page as it renders in Microsoft's Internet Explorer 5.

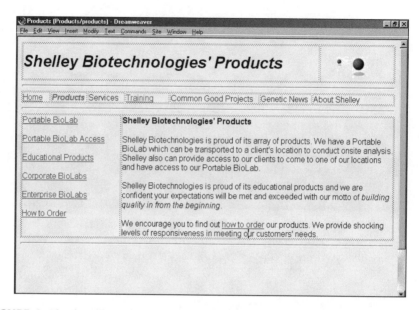

FIGURE 4–48 The Shelley Biotechnologies' Products Web page.

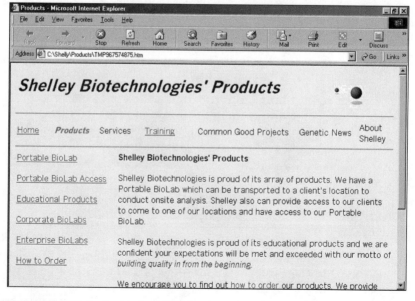

FIGURE 4–49 The Shelley Biotechnologies' Products Web page rendered in Microsoft's Internet Explorer 5.

◆ Completing the How to Order Form

The purpose of this section is to provide instructions for creating the How to Order form to enable Shelley's customers to place orders. While you will be provided with step-by-step procedures on how to create the How to Order form, you will be creating the Build Your Training Schedule form without detailed step-by-step procedures. You will learn enough in creating the How to Order form so that you can successfully create the Build Your Training Schedule form on your own.

In the following procedure, certain insertions, such as the horizontal rule, are not going to be spelled out. It is assumed that you will format the How to Order form consistent with the other Web pages you have developed.

Follow these steps to create the How to Order form.

1. View the final How to Order form at *http://www.phptr.com/ essential* to see how your work will look when finished.
2. Bring up the skeletal How to Order form in Dreamweaver 3, shown in Figure 4–50.

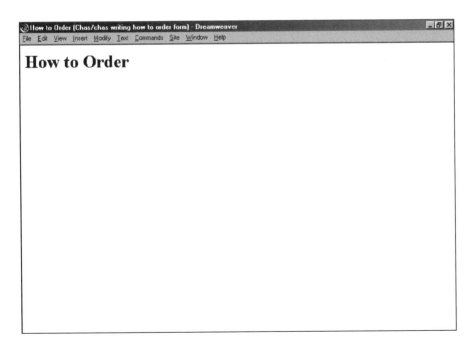

FIGURE 4–50 The skeletal How to Order form.

3. Change the Heading 1 style of the How to Order form to be consistent with the Web pages you have created thus far.

4. Access the **logo.gif** and insert it in the appropriate place to the right of the Heading 1.

5. Insert the horizontal text hyperlinks, representing links to pages at the same level, across the page, applying the styling and placement you have followed thus far.

6. Insert a Heading 2, call it *Instructions*, and press **Enter**.

7. Insert the following sentence and press **Enter**.

   Complete the form below to order Shelley Biotechnologies' products or services.

8. Insert a two-column table for spacing, as you did previously.

9. Insert parent and child text hyperlinks into the left column as you have done previously.

10. Insert a Heading 3 called *Personal Information* into the right column of the table you created in step 8, and press **Enter**.

11. Insert a two-column, seven-row table into the right column of the table you created in step 8.

    Result: You now have a table within a table.

12. Follow the table below to create the field labels and the number of positions in the text field in the left column and right column of the table respectively.

Field Label	Number of Positions
Name	40
Street Address	60
City	40
State	Field default
Zip Code	Field default
Day Phone No.	40
Night Phone No.	40

13. Insert a horizontal rule followed by a Heading 3 called *Company Information* and press **Enter**.

14. Insert a two-column, eight-row table into the right column of the table you created in step 8.

15. Follow the table below to create the field labels and the number of positions in the text field in the left column and right column of the table, respectively.

Field Label	Number of Positions
Company Name	60
Your Title	60
Company Street Address	60
City	40
State	Field default
Zip Code	Field default
Company Telephone No.	40
Your E-Mail Address	40

16. Insert a horizontal rule followed by a Heading 3 called *Order Information* and press **Enter**.
17. Insert a two-column, one row table with a width of 45 percent.
18. In the left column of the table created in step 17, enter *Product* with the appropriate styling you have used thus far.
19. Be sure your mouse pointer is in the right column of the same table.
20. On the menu bar, select **Insert→Form Object→List/ Menu**.

    Result: A **message box** appears, as shown in Figure 4–51, asking if you wish to add a form tag.

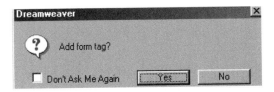

FIGURE 4–51 The Add form tag? message box.

21. Select **Don't Ask Me Again** and click the **Yes** button.
22. The List/Menu widget appears in the right column of the table.

    Figure 4–52 shows how your table should look.

Product:	Portable BioLab ▼

FIGURE 4–52 Your table should contain the List/Menu widget.

23. Click once on the **List/Menu** widget.

Result: The Properties Inspector for the List/Menu widget shows the specific properties for this widget.

24. Type *Products* in the List/Menu text box.

25. Select the **Menu** option button for **Type**.

26. Click on the **List Values** button, which is in the top right of the Properties Inspector.

Result: The **List Values** dialog box appears, as shown in Figure 4–53.

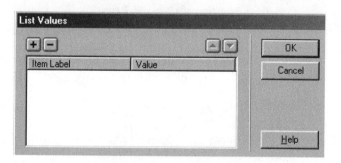

FIGURE 4–53 The List Values dialog box.

27. Enter the following labels into the Item Label, column pressing **tab** twice to advance to the next line.

The item labels are:

- *Portable BioLab*
- *Portable BioLab Access*
- *Educational Products*
- *Corporate BioLabs*
- *Enterprise BioLabs*

Figure 4–54 shows the completely entered list of values.

28. Click the **OK** button.

Result: The List Values dialog box closes and the entered values appear in the Initially Selected Open Selection List of the Properties Inspector, shown in Figure 4–55.

29. If necessary, press **Enter** to proceed to a new line.

30. Type a Heading 3 called *Credit Card Information* and press **Enter**.

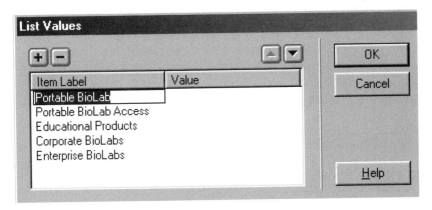

FIGURE 4–54 The List Values dialog box with all item labels entered.

31. Insert a two-column, three-row table with a width of 45 percent.

32. In the left column, first row, type Credit Card, followed by a full colon.

33. Apply the appropriate CSS styling to Credit Card.

34. Right justify Credit Card and change the cell alignment of Credit Card to **top**.

35. Place your mouse pointer in the right cell of the first row.

36. On the menu bar, select **Insert→Form Object→ RadioButton**.

Result: A RadioButton is inserted in the right cell of the first row, and the Properties Inspector is changed to show the RadioButton attributes.

37. In the RadioButton text box, type Credit, in the Checked-Value text box type *Visa;* and for the Initial State select **Checked**.

38. To the right of the RadioButton you inserted in steps 36 and 37, type the text label *Visa* and press **Enter**.

FIGURE 4–55 The Initially Selected Open Selection List of the Properties Inspector.

39. On the menu bar, select **Insert→Form Object→Radio-Button**.

Result: A RadioButton is inserted in the right cell of the second row and the Properties Inspector is changed to show the RadioButton attributes.

40. In the RadioButton text box, type *Credit* (which is the Group Name); in the CheckedValue text, box type *MC;* and for the Initial State, select **Unchecked.**

41. To the right of the RadioButton you inserted in steps 39 and 40, type the text label *Master Card* and press **Enter**.

42. On the menu bar, select **Insert→Form Object→ RadioButton**.

Result: A RadioButton is inserted in the right cell of the third row and the Properties Inspector is changed to show the RadioButton attributes.

43. In the RadioButton text box, type *Credit* (which is the Group Name); in the CheckedValue text box type *AE;* and for the Initial State, select **Unchecked.**

44. To the right of the RadioButton you inserted in steps 42 and 43, type the text label *American Express* and press **Enter**.

45. In the first column, second row, type *Credit Card No.,* followed by a full colon.

46. Right justify Credit Card No. and change the cell alignment of Credit Card to **top**.

CAUTION:
Do not assume that because the label Credit Card No. appears as properly aligned in the document window, that this will hold true in browsers. You want to make sure **Credit Card No.** will align properly when various browsers render it.

---

47. Place your mouse pointer in the right cell of the second row.

48. On the menu bar, select **Insert→Form Object→Text Field**.

Result: A text field of the default size is inserted in the right cell of the second row.

49. In the Property Inspector, type *Cr_Cd_No2* in the TextField, make the character width 40, and leave the Type as **Single line**.

50. In the left cell of the third row of the same table, type *Expiration Date,* followed by a full colon, and right-align the text.

51. Place your mouse pointer in the right cell of the third row.

52. Type the word *Month* followed by one space.

53. On the menu bar, select **Insert→Form Object→List/Menu**.

54. In the Property Inspector, type *Exp Date* in the List/Menu text box.

55. Click on the **List Values** button, which is in the top right of the Properties Inspector.

56. Enter the numerals 1 through 12, representing the months, into the Item Label column, pressing tab twice to advance to the next line. Figure 4–56 shows the completed Property Inspector for Month.

FIGURE 4–56 The completed Property Inspector for Month.

57. To the right of the List/Menu for Month, type *Year,* followed by a single space.

58. On the menu bar, select **Insert→Form Object→List/Menu**.

59. In the Property Inspector, type *Year* in the List/Menu text box.

60. Click on the **List Values** button, which is in the top right of the Property Inspector.

61. Enter the following labels into the **Item Label** column, pressing **tab** twice to advance to the next line.

The item labels are:

- 2000
- 2001
- 2002
- 2003
- 2004
- 2005

62. Click **OK**.

63. If necessary, press **Enter** and insert a horizontal rule.

64. Place the mouse pointer below the horizontal rule inserted in step 63.

65. Insert a two-column, one-row table with a width of 45 percent.

66. Place your mouse pointer in the first column.

67. On the menu bar, select **Insert→Form Object→Button**.

Result: A button called **Submit** is inserted in the first column.

NOTE:

No changes need to be made to the button properties.

---

68. Place your mouse pointer in the right column of the table.

69. On the menu bar, select **Insert→Form Object→Button**.

Result: A button called **Submit** is inserted in the right column.

70. On the Property Inspector, select **Reset**.

Result: The button is renamed **Reset**.

71. On the Property Inspector, change the **Button Name** to **Reset**.

72. If necessary, press **Enter** and insert a horizontal line.

73. Check the How to Order form in your browser and make any adjustments required.

A partial screen snapshot of the completed form is shown in Figure 4–57. You are encouraged to compare your solution to the one on the companion Shelley Web site *http://www.phptr.com/ essential*.

◆ Next Step: Completing Development of Your Training Pages

We have now completed the development of all of the Product pages. Your next step is to complete the development of the Training pages, including the Build Your Training Schedule form.

Follow these steps to complete development of your Training pages.

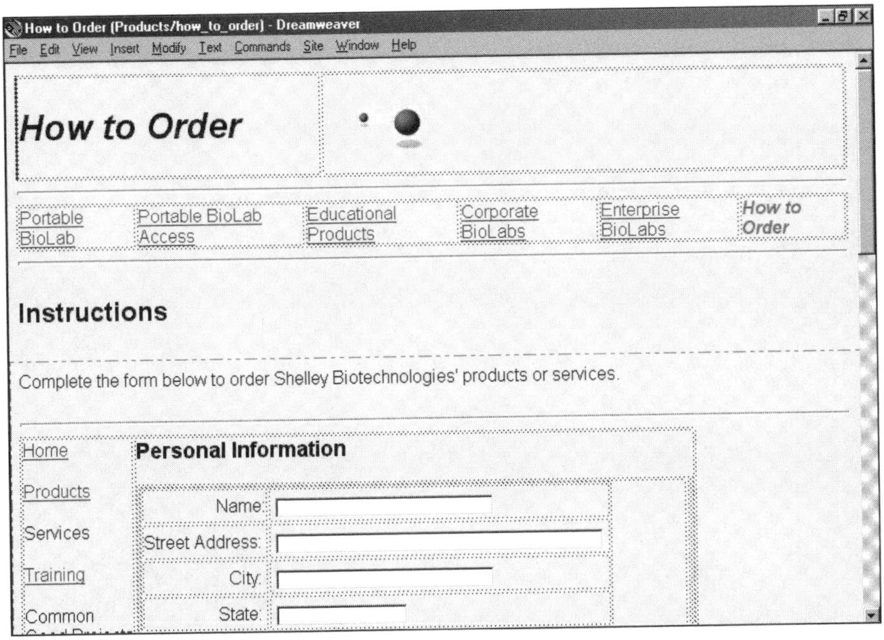

FIGURE 4–57 A partial screen snapshot of the How to Order form.

1. Using what you have learned so far, complete the development of all the training pages including the Build Your Training Schedule form.

HINT:
Use the How to Order form as a model for creating the Build Your Training Schedule form.

2. Check your work in your browser after you complete this assignment.

◆ Shelley Biotechnolgies Wrap-up

By now, you should have designed the entire Shelley Biotechnologies Web site, following the examples shown at the Companion Web site *(http://www.phptr.com/essential).* You should review your entire design in your browser. In the following chapters of this book, you will learn principles and guidelines which you can apply to the Shelley project.

Notes

1. *Macromedia Dreamweaver 3: Using Dreamweaver,* (San Francisco: Macromedia, Inc. 1999), 9.
2. Ibid., 21–60.

5 General Guidelines

IN THIS CHAPTER

- Audience
- Navigation
- Content
- Web Pages
- Quality
- Security

◆ Audience

Audience for Shelley Biotechnologies

In the Analysis Phase of the Web development process, we defined our audience for the Shelley site. We saw that Shelley's audience consisted of

- Customers
- Financial analysts
- Scientists
- Students
- Business people
- Vendors
- Competitors

Audience Background

You will remember that for each particular audience, we wanted further information regarding

- Interests, needs, skills, capabilities, and assumptions
- Platform, browser, application connection speed, and degree of Net savvy and experience
- Platform descriptions to include make, models, RAM, hard drives, CD-ROM, and data load for each[1]

Let's take one audience, customers, and look at specific information for each category. Table 5–1 shows the specific information for each category.

TABLE 5–1 Audience Background: Customers

Information Category	Specific Information
Interests, needs, skills, capabilities, and assumptions	Sophisticated business, educational, and scientific people who are highly capable.
	Need product, service, and training information, and need to do research.
	Global audience.
Platform, browser, application connection speed, and degree of Net savvy and experience	Likely to have latest state-of-the-art platforms with relatively high connection speeds.
	Audience most likely has Net savvy and experience.
Platform descriptions to include make, models, RAM, hard drives, CD-ROM, and data load for each	Hardware/software platforms used will vary, i.e., Windows, UNIX, LINUX, Macintosh.
	Likely to have relatively high RAM, large hard drives, and CD-ROM capabilities.

With our audience background fully in mind, let us now take a look at guidelines that impact the usability of the Shelley Biotechnologies Web site for our audience.

Minimalist Approach

For a global audience, there is a great benefit in taking a minimalist approach in building Shelley's Web site. A minimalist approach says that we are going to use the simplest techniques and tools in building the site. We will build our site so that it is more likely to render on most browsers. This means using HTML tags that are not browser-specific. Since we are using Macromedia

Dreamweaver 3 as our Web creation tool, it is likely that the HTML code generated by Dreamweaver 3 will not be specific to any particular browser, and will render appropriately on all of the browsers our audience uses.

Additionally, Web sites that are built taking the minimalist approach and using Dreamweaver 3 are easier to maintain. Sites that are built with too many bells and whistles are generally more difficult to maintain.

Avoid Browser-Specific Tags

Avoid browser-specific tags. For example, Internet Explorer supports the marquee tag, <MARQUEE>. However, Netscape, as well as other browsers, does not support this tag. In Internet Explorer, the marquee tag scrolls text across the page, but when testing this tag in Netscape, the desired effect of text scrolling across the page does not occur.

Narrow Bandwidth

Because of the international audience, we need to focus closely on bandwidth. Some countries do not have the robust infrastructure of hardware and software required to support extensive use of graphics. Consequently, we may need to go lean with graphics, since bandwidth will be an issue in some areas of the world. And yet, to adequately show the full array of Shelley's products, services, and research, we certainly would want to use photographs and other graphics. One option is to provide a text-only alternative for areas of the world where bandwidth is a more serious issue.

Additionally, one can often use drawings instead of photographs to illustrate the relevant features of a particular product. Photographs frequently show too much granularity and detail that is not needed to understand a particular idea or concept. Macromedia's Flash[2] enables the use of vector graphics, based on mathematical formulas. Drawings rendered as vector graphics take up much less memory and storage than do raster graphics, and can transmit more quickly.

Language Translation

Another factor regarding the international audience is that not all languages read left to right. Some languages read right to left. And some languages, such as, Japanese, use different characters. Japanese and Chinese characters tend to be larger than letter-based languages.

And when languages are translated, words in English will often expand in European languages, and tables may overflow.

For Web sites that are deployed on an extensive global basis, it is recommended that all of the unique physical representations, such as date and time, be represented in separate resource files with the main program accessing each of these different files as needed. One should not code into the mainline program all of the unique ways information can be represented. Maintaining such a program would be extremely difficult. However, making changes to separate resource files for various countries is relatively easy.

Icons

The use of icons[3] for an international audience may be problematic. Icons that Americans may view as appropriate may be offensive to those of a different culture.

When using icons, be sure to show both the icon and the text name, or label, for the icon. Also, *do not* embed the icon label into the icon image. Show the icon label as separate text and leave enough room for translation overflow.

Be sure to test your icons with people who are familiar with different cultures, or with colleagues who are from the cultures representing your international audience.

Maximize Efficacy

We can ensure that a Web site will be of tremendous value to our customers by

- providing usable, well-organized content
- minimizing the size of our content and the time it takes for the content to load for the customer.

◆ Navigation

Making the Site Visible

When a user accesses your Web site, the overall architecture of the site should be visible to her. In reality, whatever users' eyes rest on should not be overwhelming. You can manage the size of the site by employing the principles[4] discussed earlier:

- Chunking
- Relevance

- Labeling
- Consistency

Chapter 3, "Design," treats this subject in detail. By applying these simple principles in your design, you end up with a site that a visitor will want to bookmark. The fundamental reason is that the user perceives value in the site. Additionally, there is nothing in this overall view that violates perceptual or short-term memory limits (see Chapter 2, "Analysis").

Links

We have talked previously about consistency in the way links are portrayed. If you use a green Help button in the lower right bottom of the screen, your user is going to expect to find this exact representation for Help on each and every page in the site. If on a whim, you decide to occasionally sprinkle in some Help hyperlinks as pure text hyperlinks (Help) and put these in different places on different pages, your user will get frustrated. Credibility is lost because you chose to *use a difference where there was no difference.* Your readers look for patterns. When they see a break in pattern for no good reason, they get frustrated and exit the site.

It matters less whether you choose to use a green Help button or a simple text Help hyperlink. But whatever you choose, be consistent and use the same representation in the same screen location, throughout your site. Actually, plain text Help hyperlinks render quickly compared to graphic Help buttons, which may render more slowly.

Make your links intuitive. For example,

New XML Tools now available.

Avoid having too much text in the hyperlink. For example,

An article by J.R. Smith was published in the *Review of Web Products.* This article details the advantages and disadvantages of using the professional version of *Genesis II.* This software makes the development and publication of XML documents intuitive. However, the inclusion of this intuitivity sacrifices some of the robust features found in other similar products.

Avoid having small hyperlinks that are hard to see and click on. For example,

LINUX is a UNIX-based operating system for PCs. It is getting rave reviews.

Context

Navigation Questions. As we saw in Chapter 3, people using a Web site need to have a context of where they are. You will remember that they need to be able to answer the following questions.[5]

- Where am I?
- Where can I go?
- How can I get there?
- How can I get back?

BOOKS VS. ONLINE WEB PAGES

Actually, we need to answer these questions whether we are reading a book or an online Web page. With a book, it is a lot easier to find our way around. First, we have been reading books since we were small children. We can navigate by simply flipping pages. There is usually a table of contents and, hopefully, an index. We can use yellow stickies to mark pages,[6] and we can lay out several books at a time on a desk in front of us.

However, with a Web site, things are not so easy. All we have in front of us is the two-dimensional screen. And this screen is one of many screens. Our ability to keep our context (where we are in relation to other pages) is challenged. But by organizing our site, as discussed earlier, and adding some navigation aids, we can help our reader move around our Web site.

NAVIGATION AIDS

To help visitors navigate your site, follow the guidelines below.

- Provide hyperlinks to the home page and other pages at the top and bottom of each page.
- Provide a site map that shows where the reader is in relation to other pages.
- Show the hyperlinks to the other pages in the site on the left of the screen, with the page content shown to the right. A two-column table without borders can be used to line up the text hyperlinks and content. You can do this without using frames if most of your content can be seen in the window, without the need to scroll. If your content goes beyond the bottom of the window, then using frames will enable the hyperlinks on the left side of the screen to remain in place while the reader scrolls the right frame containing the content.

Figure 5–1 shows the use of a two-column, borderless table to show and align text hyperlinks in the left column and content in the right column.

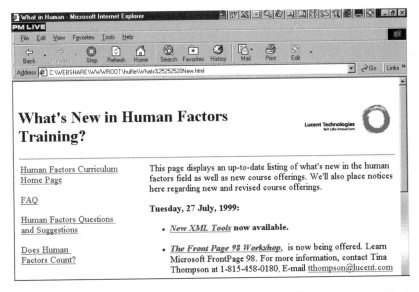

FIGURE 5–1 Example of using two-column borderless table. (*Source:* Lucent Technologies, Learning and Performance Center, Internal Human Factors Web site, 1999.)

A SIMPLE TECHNIQUE

The hyperlinks on the left side appear on every page in the site. I simply copied them over. I used a borderless table to arrange the page. The first, left-most column contains the hyperlinks. A second, skinny column appears so that when the reader reduces window size, the text and hyperlinks will not overlap. The third (right) column contains the page text.

By the way, when working on these pages, I left the table borders on. When finished, I turned the table borders off so that when the page renders in a browser, it appears without the table borders, as shown above.

FEW GRAPHICS

I have only four graphics on the entire site. One is the Lucent Technologies logo, a GIF file. The other three graphics are small JPEG photos.

A SIMPLE SITE

This site is simple and easy to maintain. All the hyperlinks are text hyperlinks. The pages load quickly on the earliest browsers and render quickly, regardless of bandwidth.

SITE MAINTENANCE

By avoiding unnecessary bells and whistles, I have saved myself a lot of grief in site maintenance.

FRAME USAGE

I chose not to use frames for the Human Factors Curriculum Web site because it was clear to me that I could provide optimal navigation without them. Tim Berners-Lee did a great service by coming up with the Web page concept.[7] A Uniform Resource Locator (URL) guarantees a unique occurrence of a particular Web page. With the introduction of frame technology, we are dividing up our window, or Web page, into subpages, each with its own scrolling capability and its own navigation. Thus, navigation can become inconsistent. Also, I felt that it would be a lot harder to maintain the site if I employed frames.

Actually, using frames to show a table of contents in the left frame and the current window in the right frame is an effective use of frames. I simply chose to keep things simple.

◆ Content

Introduction

As we discussed earlier, people do not like to read on the Web. They would rather scan a Web page for what they need. Reading from screens is slower than reading from paper, so we need to arrange our content in a way that entices people into our site and provides just what they need, in a simple, easy-to-find way.

Fundamental Principles

As we have seen, the following fundamental principles[8] apply to laying out content.
- Chunking
- Relevance

- Labeling
- Consistency

Since people can comfortably handle only four to six items of information in a chunk, we need to manage the size of our content throughout our Web site. Keeping relevant information together results in manageable chunks. Providing labels and other guides, such as hyperlinks and site maps, helps the reader navigate directly to the information he or she needs. Consistency in the way chunks of information are presented and in the steps the user follows to get to the information results in a site that is organized and user-friendly.

An Example

Figure 5–2 is another example from the Human Factors Curriculum Web site.

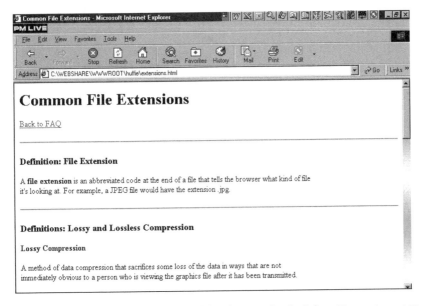

FIGURE 5–2 Example of application of fundamental principles. (*Source:* Lucent Technologies, Learning and Performance Center, Internal Human Factors Web site, 1999.)

The Common File Extensions Web page was written in simple HTML. The page was developed in response to my students requesting a list of common file extensions. Figure 5–2 shows the beginning of the Web page, where I define some terminology. Again, the information is simply presented in small bites, or chunks, so a reader can scan the page and easily find the needed information. And because it is all text, the page renders instantly.

◆ Web Pages

Introduction

My experience on the Web tells me that you have about four seconds to capture the attention of your reader on your Web page. Some things to look out for are

- Browser Fails to Render Page.
- Content Beneath the "Fold"
- Excessive Graphics
- Irrelevant Animations
- Continuous Movement
- Mixed Modalities

Each of these is treated in detail below.

Browser Fails to Render Page

Using browser-specific techniques, such as the marquee tag in Internet Explorer, will likely guarantee that your page will not render properly in other browsers. It is very important to check your Web site in all browsers that your audience will be using and in all possible versions of a given browser they might likely have.

In large organizations, the principal browsers are Internet Explorer and Netscape. One can generally count on business users in large companies, such as Lucent Technologies, having a fairly up-to-date version of these browsers. Therefore, any Web site that I develop for a large organization will be tested in both the Internet Explorer and Netscape browsers, as well as in the different versions of these browsers I am likely to encounter. Some employees have UNIX-type workstations, and so the Web site must be tested on these workstations as well.

When you go to other organizations throughout the world, the variations of browsers and browser versions can magnify. Again, if pages are developed taking a minimalist approach, it is likely that the pages will render on almost all browsers, even on text-only browsers such as Lynx.

Content Beneath the Fold

For years in newspaper publishing, it has been an axiom to put important and eye-catching information above the "fold" in the newspaper. Newspapers are displayed with the top half in view. Less critical information is put beneath the fold.

The same principle is true of a Web page. Put your important information above the "fold," that is, above the bottom of the screen window. Many people may not bother to scroll and could miss important content, such as help buttons or navigation buttons. With important information in easy view, you will ensure that your reader will not miss critical content.

Excessive Graphics

Most recently, it seems to me, companies have gone out of their way to have a lot of graphics on their Web pages. I see pages indicating that 24 graphics are loading. I have no patience to watch the countdown of graphics rendering. When bandwidth becomes irrelevant, this will not be an issue, but in the meantime, the wait can be excruciating, even on T1 lines and cable modem lines.

Any graphic shown on a Web page should have direct and real value to the reader. If a graphic adds no value to the communication, why include it? Obviously, there are cases where graphics are needed, such as for a diagram of a piece of equipment. In this case, if you are going to use the graphic repeatedly, keep it the same so it gets cached and hence renders quickly each time it is needed.

Irrelevant Animations

To me there is nothing worse than an animation that adds no value to the page. A good use of an animation would be to show a hand turning a screwdriver to put a bolt in a cabinet. To use a video to show this would take up an enormous amount of storage and computer resources. Also, the video would show too much granularity to be clear. The animation takes up less storage space and can be a simple loop to reduce file size. It has only the detail needed to enable someone to follow the instructions.

My emphasis here is chiefly on business, government, and academic sites. Sites meant to provide, for example, discovery learning for children are a different matter entirely. Use of animations on these sites may provide interest and facilitate learning.

Continuous Movement

Pages with continuous movement can be irritating and can take up resources unnecessarily. Movement distracts the reader from the task at hand. Any movement should be value-added to the tasks the user will be doing while reading the Web page.

Mixed Modalities

A real no-no is to have pages with mixed modalities that are unrelated but in action at the same time. For example, imagine a diagram of the parts of the human eye. The diagram is in motion as different parts of the eye are discussed. The discussion consists of text that appears in a typewriter fashion, say a word at a time, and does not match the motion of the diagram. Additionally, there is audio playing at the same time, and it is entirely different than the text or the diagram. Depending on the speed of the computer and the browser version, things could get further unsynchronized, causing the visitor to become frustrated and exit the site.

◆ Quality

Introduction

One often-heard definition of quality is *no hassle.* If I go out to dinner at a restaurant and at the end of the evening realize that I had no hassle, I consider the evening a "quality" one. On the other hand, if my dinner experience starts with having to wait one hour despite a reservation, I'm hassled, and that's not quality. Then, if the waiter is rude and conspicuous by his absence, I'm hassled even more, and that's not quality.

Applied to Web Sites

This same concept of quality can be applied to Web sites. If a reader can navigate and read your Web site without feeling hassled, that's quality. If, on the other hand, the same reader goes to another Web site and immediately feels overwhelmed and hassled, that's not quality.

It is interesting about quality—*I know it when I see it.*

While I realize that the above is somewhat unscientific in terms of measurable criteria, nevertheless, I think it resonates with our experience. And the way we build a quality site is to perform usability testing with valid test subjects and test criteria. As stated in Chapter 4, "Implementation and Testing," we measure by facts. We see how long it takes our test subjects to complete a transaction, and how many and what type of errors they make. We then revise our site and retest. We iterate this process until we are convinced that our site has passed our test criteria. This is where the science comes in. If we build in the science, our reader *knows quality when she sees it and does not feel hassled.*

Quality has to be built in from the very beginning. Quality is not something we can easily add after our site has been published. This is called retrofitting or reengineering. Retrofitting is very expensive and tends to have a negative effect on reputation and credibility. Taking the "prevention approach" and building quality in at the start is at least one-third less expensive than detecting and correcting errors and problems later.

Specific Testing

Before we even get to our usability testing, we want to check for the following:

- Test All Links
- Verify HTML/XML Syntax
- Test on All Relevant Browsers
- Edit Each Page

Test All Links

Testing all links is critical. Don't let your Web site readers find broken links. It will reduce your credibility with your audience. Macromedia Dreamweaver 3 has a nice feature to check for and fix broken links.

Testing Web Pages

EDIT CHECKS OF HTML/XML CODE

Edit your HTML and XML code. Avoid using browser-specific tags.

TEST ON ALL RELEVANT BROWSERS

View the rendering of your Web pages in all relevant browsers your audience is likely to use to ensure that your page is readable to your target audience. You do not want your audience to find out that the browser they have won't render your page. It is possible that another version of the same browser may render that same page. Even within the two major browsers, Internet Explorer and Netscape, there are many differences in how pages are rendered. While a Heading 1 is always a Heading 1, it may appear as Arial (sans-serif font) in one browser and as Times Roman (serif font) in another browser.

TEST EXAMPLES

Internet Explorer 3 has a gray background. Internet Explorer 4 and 5 have white backgrounds. I once had a signature GIF file that I did not make transparent because it rendered fine in Internet Explorer versions 4 and 5. Luckily, I did test the GIF in Internet Explorer 3 and found that I did not have a transparent background. I then made the GIF transparent so it would render in all browsers.

Additionally, graphics may appear differently. I once tested a graphic in Netscape and it rendered at the right size. I then tested the same graphic in Mosaic and it was the size of the whole Web page.

DON'T INTUIT

It is better not to try to intuit, based on general experience, how a given browser or a given version of a browser may render a page. You may be very surprised. The acid test way is to actually test it in that browser and in all relevant versions of that browser.

EDIT EACH PAGE

Remember to check your Web pages for typos. A good spell-checker is helpful, but it can give you false comfort. If you should type *the* rather than *their*, the spellchecker will not pick that up. So a good visual edit of your Web pages is in order. Ask a colleague who is not familiar with your content to read the pages. He or she is more likely to pick up typos. Typos and grammatical errors can affect your credibility.

Assessing Web Site Quality

There is a variety of software tools that are available to aid Web designers in assessing and maintaining the quality of their Web sites.

TRAFFIC TRACKING

Systems for tracking traffic through your site range in price from free to quite expensive. They all require attention to set up and keep running properly. A tracking system is like an accounting system: once you have collected the data, it is only as good as the reports you ask it for. Tracking software can help you understand whether you're achieving your goals or not.

TRAFFIC EVALUATION

The two things to watch when reviewing your site-traffic logs are the number of visitors coming to your front page and the ratio of visitors continuing through the site. Do most of them get to the second level, but then almost no one goes deeper? That's a sign your home page is doing its job, but your neighborhood pages are weak. Does everyone go right to one specific second-level page? If so, either strengthen that area to serve them better, or strengthen the other areas to attract more visitors, or both.

TRACKING TOOLS

Table 5–2 shows the tool name, tool description, and URL reference for two tools that are available for assessing Web site traffic, 1. 2. 3. Counter and Tracker and Web-Stat Internet Services. The tracking tool Web site examples are shown in Figures 5–3 and 5–4.

TABLE 5–2 Tracking Tools

Tool Name	Tool Description	URL Reference
1.2.3. Counter and Tracker	Offers counter with optional Web tracker, providing traffic analysis and search engine tracking.	*http://www.123count.com*
Web-Stat Internet Services	Offers Web counters and powerful statistics and log analysis tools.	*http://www.web-stat.com*

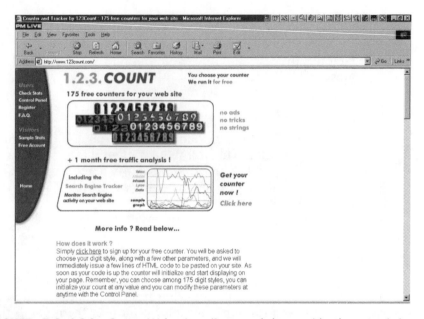

FIGURE 5–3 1.2.3. Count Web site. (Presented here with the permission of *123Count.com.*)

FIGURE 5–4 Web-Stat Web site. (Presented here with the permission of WEB-STAT Internet Services.)

◆ Security

Introduction

If you have a corporate security department or someone in your organization charged with this responsibility, you might find it helpful to have them involved in your Web site development. Corporations have definite policies regarding the protection of proprietary information. Remember that the knowledge in your business is worth a lot financially and that it took a lot of resources to develop.

Firewalls

Many organizations have firewalls, which consist of software that protects unauthorized people outside the firewall from accessing information inside the firewall. As electronic commerce gains in usage, companies are going to be allowed to access an extranet, a portion of your site within your firewall. These companies will be engaged in e-commerce, which I see as the future of the Internet.

Corporate security departments are going to implement practices and standards to ensure that a company's proprietary information is safeguarded in the e-commerce environment.

Development Standards

Many corporations today have standards in place to be followed in Web site development. There are standards as to a "common look and feel" as well as standards for the Web development process. Using a proven Web development process, or methodology, raises the odds that successful and secure Web sites will be developed.

Notes

1. Darcy DiNucci, Maria Giudice, and Lynne Stiles, *Elements of Web Design,* 2d ed. (Berkeley, Calif.: Peachpit Press, 1998), 38–41.
2. Kyle, Lynn, *Essential Flash 4 for Web Professionals* (Upper Saddle River, NJ: Prentice Hall PTR, 2000), 2.
3. Horton, William, *The Icon Book* (New York: John Wiley & Sons, Inc., 1994), 258–267.

4. Information Mapping, Inc., Internal Course Materials, 1999.

5. Ibid.

6. Ibid.

7. Nielsen, Jakob, *"Why Frames Suck (Most of the Time),"* Alertbox, December 1996, *http://www.useit.com/alertbox/9612.html.*

8. Information Mapping, Inc., Internal Course Materials, 1999.

6 Graphics

IN THIS CHAPTER

- Introduction
- File Formats
- Color
- Image Maps
- Graphics Tools

◆ Introduction

Throughout this chapter, you will be viewing images that are presented here in grayscale. You are encouraged to go to the companion Web site *http://www.phptr.com/essential* to view the images in color.

◆ File Formats

Basic Formats

The two most common graphics formats on the Web are

- GIF (Graphic Interchange Format) developed by Compu-Serve
- JPEG (Joint Photographic Experts Group) the committee that established the JPEG standard.

GIF FORMAT

The GIF format was designed for online delivery because it was originally developed by CompuServe in the late 1980s. It compresses graphics beautifully, using lossless compression, which results in no loss of image quality. GIF images work well for line drawings and solid areas of color. I have found that the GIF format renders old monochrome family photographs extremely well.

GIF89A supports animation, transparency, and interlacing. Animation consists of a graphic that moves on the screen, for example, a rotating globe. Transparency refers to making the background color of the image the same as the background color of the page. Figure 6–1 is an example of a GIF used for the Lucent Technologies logo.[1]

FIGURE 6–1 A GIF used for the Lucent Technologies logo.

In the nontransparent image, the background color of the image is retained and does not match the page background color. In the transparent image, the background color of the image and the background color of the page are identical. You are invited to access the companion Web site *http://www.phptr. com/essential* to see examples of nontransparent and transparent images.

Interlacing causes the GIF to load quickly at low or chunky resolutions, and then come into full or crisp resolution.

JPEG FORMAT

The JPEG format has a bit depth of 24 bits. JPEG was developed specifically for photographs and other images with lots of colors.

The JPEG format allows almost 17 million colors, far more than the human eye can see. JPEG is a lossy compression algorithm, meaning that information is removed from the image, thereby causing a loss in image quality. Often, the difference is not visible to the human eye and therefore not noticed by the reader. Figure 6–2 is a photo as a JPEG file.

FIGURE 6-2 A photograph as a JPEG file.

PROGRESSIVE JPEGS VERSUS STANDARD JPEGS

Progressive JPEGs allow higher compression than regular JPEGs and support interlacing. Progressive JPEG-making tools for the PC and Mac are found at *http://www.in-touch.com/pjpeg.html.* This site is shown in Figure 6–3.

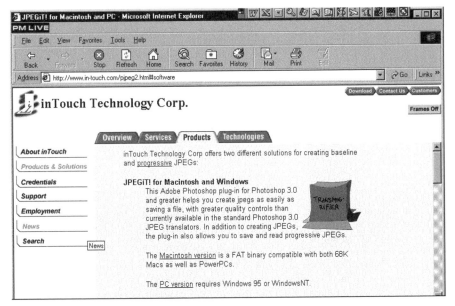

FIGURE 6-3 Site for JPEG-making Tools. Reproduced here with the permission of inTouch Technology Corporation.

NEW FORMAT: PNG

The GIF format has some limitations and may be subject to copyright restrictions. A new standard was developed to replace GIF and is called the Portable Network Graphics (PNG) specification.

The PNG format provides a portable, legally unencumbered, well-compressed, well-specified standard for lossless bitmapped image files. Although the initial motivation for developing PNG was to replace GIF, the design provides some useful new features not available in GIF, with minimal cost to developers. GIF features retained in PNG include indexed-color images of up to 256 colors, the serial reading of streamability files, progressive display, marked transparency portions of an image, complete hardware and platform independence, and effective 100 percent lossless compression.

Important new features of PNG, not available in GIF, include true-color images of up to 48 bits per pixel, image gamma information, and faster initial presentation in progressive display mode. PNG is designed to be simple, portable, and robust. The design supports full file integrity-checking as well as simple, quick detection of common transmission errors. Figure 6–4 shows an image in PNG format.

FIGURE 6–4 Image in PNG format.

◆ Color

Introduction

When designing for the Web, it is best to design for monochrome first. In other words, **get it right in black and white.** The rationale for this approach is that the developer should focus on the overall design and layout of the Web pages. Getting too caught up in color early in the project may cause retrofitting later, because the Web pages have changed dramatically and certain widgets and controls may have been added or deleted.

Once the general layout of the site's Web pages has been done, then color can be added consistently and efficiently, with no lost time. The maximum combination of colors should be four to six but it is *better* to use only three or four colors if you can. Obviously, this excludes photographs and company logos. I saw one design with only three colors used. It was very easy to keep track of the colors and their meanings. We definitely want to avoid the confusing effect of too many colors.

Keep in mind that for international sites, certain colors have stereotypical meanings. In translating from a U.S. user to a user in Saudi Arabia, for example, changing colors can be tricky. If you change a background color, you have to choose a foreground color that will contrast appropriately. If we stay with an off-white screen background with black text, we have achieved the greatest contrast possible, made the reading of the text as easy as possible, and eliminated having to translate foreground and background colors for a particular culture.

How to Use Color

Use color purposefully, consistently, sparingly to

- call attention to specific data or information
- show relationships between things
- discriminate between different areas
- help users remember
- show objects naturally and realistically
- increase visual appeal

Color Blindness

About 8 to 10 percent of the population has some form of color blindness. Of the color-blind population, approximately one half of one percent is female; the remainder is male. Keep this in mind when building your Web site.

Colors Associated with Various Cultures

Table 6–1 shows how various colors are perceived in different cultures.

TABLE 6–1 Colors Associated with Various Cultures

Culture	Red	Blue	Green	Yellow	White
United States	Danger	Masculinity	Safety	Cowardice	Purity
France	Aristocracy	Freedom Peace	Criminality	Temporary	Neutrality
Egypt	Death	Virtue Faith Truth	Fertility Strength	Happiness Prosperity	Joy
India	Life Creativity	--	Prosperity Fertility	Success	Death Purity
Japan	Anger Danger	Villainy	Future Youth Energy	Grace Nobility	Death
China	Happiness	Heaven Clouds	Ming Dynasty Heavens Clouds	Birth Wealth Power	Death Purity

(*Source:* Human Factors Curriculum, Learning and Performance Center, Lucent Technologies, 1999)

Color Wheel and Color Triangle and Color

Figure 6–5 shows the color wheel and color triangle[2] in grayscale. These are useful to reference when considering colors. You are encouraged to view the color version at *http://www.phptr.com/essential.*

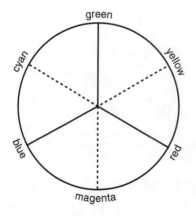
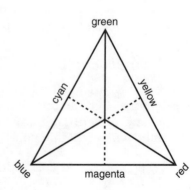

FIGURE 6–5 Color wheel and color triangle.

Avoid displaying highly saturated colors from opposite extremes of the visual spectrum. For example, red and blue mixed together can cause chromosteropsis. If a person stares at a particular color for an extended period, then the cones in the eye for that color wear out and cones representing colors at the opposite end of the color spectrum kick in.

◆ An Experiment

You are encouraged to proceed to the companion Web site *http://www.phptr.com/essential* to perform an experiment on perceiving colors. The results of the experiment are discussed on the Web site.

Background and Foreground Contrast

While hue (the light frequency of a color) and saturation (the purity of a color) are indeed important, contrast is even more important for reading text. Contrast is the lightness difference between foreground and background.

In the example in Figure 6–6, the black text on an off-white background provides the greatest contrast. Again, you are encouraged to visit the companion Web site where an expanded color version of Figure 6–6 is presented, showing both black text on an off-white background and green text on a magenta background. You can see how dramatically poor the contrast is when colors are carelessly selected.

◆ Image Maps

Image maps are portions of images that are hypertext links. Using a mouse-based Web client such as Netscape or Internet Explorer, the user clicks on different parts of a mapped image to

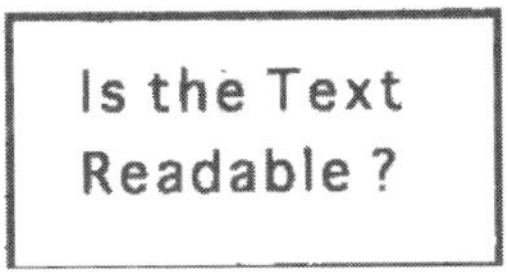

Is the Text
Readable ?

FIGURE 6–6 Background and foreground contrast.

activate different hypertext links. An example of an image map is shown in Figure 6–7.

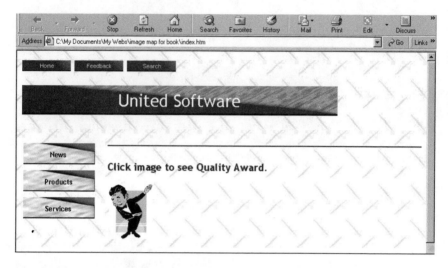

FIGURE 6–7 Example of image map.

In Figure 6–7, the entire image is an image map. The reader can click on any portion of the image and see United Software's quality award.

◆ Graphics Tools

There are a number of graphics tools available. These include

- Adobe's Photoshop, Go Live, and ImageStyler
- inTouch Technology's JPEG Transmogrifier
- Macromedia's Fireworks and Flash

Notes

1. Lucent Technologies, Learning and Performance Center, Internal Human Factors Web site, 1999.
2. Fortner, Brand and Theodore E. Meyer, *Number by Colors: A Guide to Using Color to Understand Technical Data* (New York: Springer-Verlag, 1997), 91.

7 Accessible Design for Users with Disabilities

◆ Introduction

Jakob Nielsen, in his Alertboxes,[1,2] offers comprehensive information about Web design for disabled users, which is summarized in this chapter.

The National Institute on Disability and Rehabilitation Research's Rehabilitation Engineering Research Center for Access to Computers and Information Systems has published a comprehensive set of guidelines for accessible Web design. More details can be found in those guidelines.

◆ Americans with Disabilities Act

A text copy of the Americans with Disabilities Act, August 1992, can be found at *gopher://wiretap.spies.com/00/Gov/disable.act.*

The Department of Justice's ADA homepage is found at *http://www.usdoj.gov/crt/ada/adahom1.htm* and is shown in Figure 7–1. This site is a useful resource for technical assistance and provides a search capability for the ADA Web site.

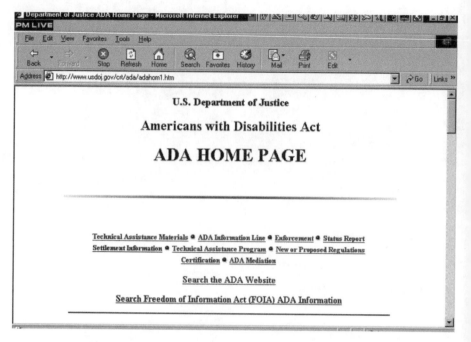

FIGURE 7-1 ADA homepage.

Web Access Symbol

The symbol shown in Figure 7–2 can be used to signify sites or pages for which an effort has been made to enhance access for disabled users. A color version of this Web Access Symbol can be found on the companion Web site.

FIGURE 7-2 Web Access Symbol.

◆ Categories of Disabilities

Disabilities can be categorized as follows:

- Visual disabilities
- Auditory disabilities
- Motor disabilities
- Cognitive disabilities

Visual Disabilities

The most serious accessibility problems, given the current state of the Web, probably relate to blind users and users with other visual disabilities, since most Web pages are highly visual. For example, it is quite common to see combinations of background and foreground colors that make pages virtually unreadable for color-blind users. Textual pages are reasonably easy for blind users to access, since the text can be fed to a screen reader.

In order to facilitate scanning, it is recommended to emphasize the structure of the page by proper HTML markup by using:

<H1> for the highest level heading
<H2> for the main parts of the information within the <H1>s
<H3> and lower levels for even finer divisions of the information

When proper HTML markup is used, the blind user can get an overview of the structure of a page by having the <H1>s and <H2>s read aloud and can quickly skip an uninteresting section by instructing the screen reader to jump to the next lower-level heading.

Most people already know about the use of ALT tags to provide alternative text for images. Some accessibility specialists advocate so-called described images, where text is provided to verbalize what a seeing user would see. For example, the Web Access Symbol shown in Figure 8–2 might be described as "a glowing globe with a keyhole."

Better still is to verbalize the meaning or role of the image in the dialog, by describing the intent of the image and what happens when the image is clicked.

Reduced Eyesight Users

In addition to completely blind users, there are many users who can see, but have reduced eyesight. These users typically need large fonts, which is a standard feature of most Web browsers. To support these users, never encode information with absolute font sizes, but use relative sizes instead.

Full support of users with reduced eyesight would require pages to look equally well at all font sizes. Doing so is often not practical, and it might be acceptable to make pages look slightly worse at huge font sizes, as long as the basic page layout will still work.

It is recommended to test pages with the default font set to 10, 12, and 14 points to ensure that the design is optimal for these common font sizes. Then make additional checks with default fonts of 18 and 24 points to make sure that the design still works at these accessibility-enhancing sizes.

Auditory Disabilities

People who are deaf or have other auditory disabilities rarely have problems on the Web, since sound effects are usually gratuitous. The usability of a site almost always stays the same when the sound is turned off. With the trend toward more multimedia, this will change. In particular, transcripts of spoken audio clips and videos should be made available in versions with subtitles (which will also benefit users who are not native speakers of the language used in the video).

Motor Disabilities

Many users have difficulty with detailed mouse movements and may also have problems holding down multiple keyboard keys simultaneously. Most of these issues should be taken care of by improved browser design and should not concern content designers, except for the advice not to design image maps that require extremely precise mouse positioning.

Cognitive Disabilities

By cognitive disabilities, we are not referring to below-average intelligence, though many sites will have to support such users as broader segments of the population go online. Unfortunately, cognitive disabilities have not been the focus of as much user interface research as have physical disabilities.

People vary in their spatial reasoning skills and in their short-term memory capacity. Programmers and graphic designers tend to get uncommonly high scores on tests of spatial reasoning skills, and are therefore good at visualizing the structure of a Web site.

Similarly, young people (i.e., most Web designers) generally have better memories for obscure codes (e.g., a URL) than older people do. It is safe to assume that most users will have significantly greater difficulty navigating a Web site than its designers will have. Specific and clear navigation helps all users.

People who have difficulty visualizing the structure of information can be helped if the site designers have produced such visualization for them in the form of a site map. They would be further aided if the browser updated the display of the site map with the path of navigation and the location of the current page.

Users with dyslexia may have problems reading long pages and will be helped if the design facilitates scanning by proper use of HTML headings. Selecting words with high information content as hypertext anchors will help these users, as well as blind users, scan for interesting links (no "click here," please). Most search interfaces require the user to type in keywords as search terms.

Users with spelling disabilities (and foreign-language users) will obviously often fail to find what they need, as long as perfect spellings are required. A first suggestion is for search engines to include a spelling checker. Other ideas such as advanced information retrieval, like query-by-example, and similarity searches, can also help these users (and benefit everybody else at the same time).

Notes

1. Nielsen, Jakob, "Accessible Design for Users with Disabilities," *Alertbox,* October 1996, *http://www.useit.com/alertbox/9610.html.*
2. Nielsen, Jakob, "Disabled Accessibility: The Pragmatic Approach," *Alertbox,* June 13, 1999, *http://www.useit.com/alertbox/990613.html.*

8 Advanced Web Design Using Extensible Markup Language (XML)

IN THIS CHAPTER

- Introduction to XML
- Comparing HTML and XML
- XML Design Goals
- Virtual Writing, Media Notwithstanding™
- XML Parsers
- Legacy Information
- Where is XML Going?
- XML and XHTML Specifications

◆ Introduction to XML

In the Beginning

Prior to the early 1980s, the Internet was command-line based, using strange-sounding commands with a UNIX flavor, such as Archie and Veronica. This was the legacy from the early use of the Internet by the military and universities. When Tim Berners-Lee conceived the idea of the Web page, with a unique Uniform Resource Locator (URL) as a Web page identifier, a whole new world opened up. To enable information to be intelligibly rendered on a Web page, varying hardware and software notwithstanding, a tagging language was needed. Thus Hypertext

Markup Language (HTML) was born. Based on Standard Generalized Markup Language (SGML), which was conceived and published in 1986 as a standard (ISO 8879), HTML provided tags, which could define the structure of a document.

Enter HTML

To those familiar with the NROFF and TROFF tagging scripts of UNIX's early text editor, the HTML tags appear similar. The Web page is not What You See Is What You Get (WYSIWYG). In HTML, tags enclosed in brackets are used to define the structure of a document. For example, <HEAD> indicates a heading, and <BODY> the body of a document. Moreover, within the body of a document, there are <P> tags denoting paragraphs. Note, however, that these tags do not tell you anything about the content of the document. So all paragraphs are defined with a <P> tag, but the tag does not tell you that this paragraph is, for example, a computer security policy, another a recipe for chocolate chip cookies. In other words, there is no content about the content, or metalanguage.

Why a Metalanguage?

Why would the lack of a metalanguage be an issue? With the advent of e-business and e-commerce, a method is needed to identify information in such a way as to enable companies to automatically request and track shipments from a vendor, authorize billings, and so on. While HTML is great for rendering a Web page, it has limitations, especially in the handling of legacy information. Without XML, is impossible for companies to read data from their legacy systems. XML identifies content in a way that no other tool can do.

◆ Comparing HTML AND XML

The best way to explain XML and its usefulness is to compare it with HTML. To do so, let's consider the need to document a catalog of books. First, we will look at how we would do this in HTML. Then we will render the same requirement in XML.

HTML Scripting

Figure 8–1 shows a simple book catalog scripted in HTML.

```
<HTML>
<HEAD>
<TITLE>Catalog</TITLE>
</HEAD>
<BODY>
<TABLE BORDER="2" BGCOLOR="white">
<TR>
  <TH>Title</TH>
  <TH>Author</TH>
</TR>
<TR>
<TD>Flash 4 for Web Professionals</TD>
<TD>Lynn Kyle</TD>
</TR>
</TABLE>
</BODY>
</HTML>
```

FIGURE 8–1 HTML script of book catalog.

When the script in Figure 8–1 is read by a browser, such as Internet Explorer or Netscape Communicator, the Web page shown in Figure 8–2 below is rendered.

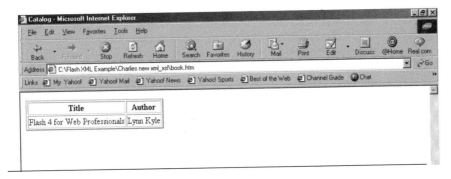

FIGURE 8–2 Book catalog rendered as a result of HTML code.

XML Scripting

Figure 8–3 shows the same book catalog scripted in XML.

```
<?xml version="1.0" encoding="ISO8859-1"?>
<?xml-stylesheet type="text/xsl" href="book.xsl"?>
<CATALOG>
  <BOOK>
        <TITLE>Flash 4 for Web Professionals</TITLE>
        <AUTHOR>Lynn Kyle</AUTHOR>
        <COUNTRY>USA</COUNTRY>
        <PUBLISHER>Prentice Hall PTR</PUBLISHER>
        <PRICE>29.99</PRICE>
        <YEAR>2000</YEAR>
  </BOOK>
</CATALOG>
```

FIGURE 8–3 XML script of book catalog.

Comparison: HTML and XML Scripts

As we have seen, the HTML code simply addresses the structure of the content of the book catalog, but the XML code tells you what the content is about. In XML, you can create your own tags, which define very specifically the nature of the content. XML is truly extensible in that it extends the capabilities of HTML.

Rendering XML in a Browser

To render XML in a browser, we need to add one more thing: Extensible Stylesheet Language (XSL). XSL stylesheets enable XML to be read in a browser program. The beauty of XML and XSL is that you can write once in XML and render many different representations of the same content with XSL.

Figure 8–4 shows the XSL style sheet code for the book catalog.

```
<?xml version="1.0"?>
<xsl:stylesheet xmlns:xsl="http://www.w3.org/TR/WD-xsl">
   <xsl:template match="/">
      <html>
         <body>
            <table border="2" bgcolor="white">
               <tr>
                  <th>Title</th>
                  <th>Author</th>
               </tr>
               <xsl:for-each select="CATALOG/BOOK">
                  <tr>
```

FIGURE 8–4 XSL stylesheet code for book catalog.

```
                    <td>
                        <xsl:value-of select="TITLE"/>
                    </td>
                    <td>
                        <xsl:value-of select="AUTHOR"/>
                    </td>
                </tr>
            </xsl:for-each>
        </table>
    </body>
</html>
    </xsl:template>
</xsl:stylesheet>
```

FIGURE 8–4 (Continued)

The Final Result: XML and XSL

Figure 8–5 shows a Web page for the book catalog rendered as a result of the XML and XSL code.

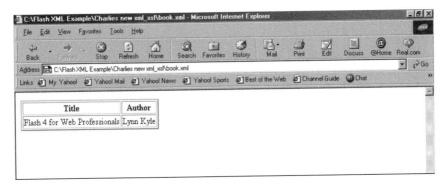

FIGURE 8–5 Book catalog rendered as a result of the XML and XSL code.

As you can see, the Web page renders just as it did with HTML. However, there is one important difference. With XML, we have now captured content about the content. We know that *Flash 4 for Web Professionals* is a book title because of the self-describing XML Title <TITLE> tag, which is far more descriptive than the table data <TD> tag used in HTML.

◆ XML Design Goals

The following ten design goals have been established for XML.

1. XML shall be straightforwardly usable over the Internet.
2. XML shall support a wide variety of applications.
3. XML shall be compatible with SGML.
4. It shall be easy to write programs that process XML documents.
5. The number of optional features in XML is to be kept to the absolute minimum, ideally zero.
6. XML documents should be human-legible and reasonably clear.
7. The XML design should be prepared quickly.
8. The design of XML shall be formal and concise.
9. XML documents shall be easy to create.
10. Terseness in XML markup is of minimal importance.

◆ Virtual Writing, Media Notwithstanding

Introduction

For some time now, I have been telling my students in all my classes that writing and Web development are changing forever. For writing, whether for paper, Web publication, online help, or for any medium, there is a need today to perform *Virtual Writing, Media Notwithstanding*. This is a phrase that I have created and trademarked.

Definition

Virtual Writing, Media Notwithstanding[1] is a business and technical writing approach that:

- Focuses on writing clear and specific content in short groups or paragrahs containing a specific heading or label
- Supports writing once, and presenting many different ways
- Emphasizes simple, specific text suitable for
  - Written translation to languages throughout the world
  - Conversion to speech for languages throughout the world

- Supports the following:
  o Unicode
  o Information Mapping®^{2}
  o XML and XHTML

◆ XML Parsers

Definition: XML Parser

An *XML parser* is a program that reads XML documents and verifies whether they are valid and well-formed. There are two types of XML parsers:

- Nonvalidating XML parser
- Validating XML parser

Definition: Nonvalidating XML Parser

A *nonvalidating XML parser* is one that checks whether XML documents are well-formed, but not whether they are valid. A well-formed document is one wherein all markup, character data, and comments must adhere to rules. Additionally, the tags and character data must relate to each other in accordance with the following set of rules:

- The document must start with an XML declaration.
- Elements that contain character data or other elements must have matching start and end tags.
- Tags denoting empty elements must end with />.
- The document must contain exactly one element that completely contains all other elements.
- Elements may nest but may not overlap.
- The characters < and & may only be used to start tags and entities, respectively.
- The only entity references that appear are &, <, >, ', and ".

Examples: Nonvalidating XML Parsers

Examples of nonvalidating XML parsers are

- HEX
- TclXML

Definition: Validating XML Parser

A *validating XML parser* is one that checks to determine whether XML documents conform to all the rules expressed in the document type definition (DTD).

Examples: Validating XML Parsers

Examples of validating XML parsers follow:

- IBM'S XML for C++ Parser (IBM's XML4C)
- XML Parser
- Sun's Java Project X
- XML for Java

◆ Legacy Information

One of the challenging areas for XML is how to deal with legacy information files. Many companies have legacy systems that may have been developed, for example, in the 1960s. The files of these legacy systems are unintelligible to today's systems unless given structure, such as the structure provided by XML.

Robert C. Lyons of Unidex, Inc. has developed XML Convert 2.0, a Java application that uses XFlat schemas to convert flat files into XML, and vice versa. XML Convert can also convert a flat file from one format to another. XML Convert 2.0 is available for purchase and a free evaluation copy is available for download at *http://www.unidex.com/xflat.htm*. Figure 8–6 shows the XML Convert Web site.

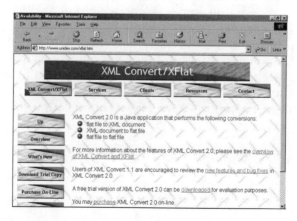

FIGURE 8–6 XML Convert Web Site. Presented here with the express permission of Unidex, Inc.

◆ Where is XML Going?

XML is becoming the foundation for the next generation of Web applications and specifications. Areas where XML has an impact include

- Publishing
- Electronic commerce

◆ XML and XHTML Specifications

The current XML 1.0 Specification is provided in Appendix C. Appendix D contains the XHTML Specification 1.0. It defines XHTML 1.0, which is a reformulation of HTML 4, as an XML 1.0 application. Basically, XHTML makes Web pages more extensible by allowing them to assimilate markup tags from XML-based languages. XHTML will also enforce discipline on HTML, insisting that, for example, closing tags be used for all tags.

Note

1. Virtual Writing, Media Notwithstanding™ is a trademark of Tektrain, Inc.
2. Information Mapping is a registered trademark of Information Mapping, Inc.

A Recommended Reading

◆ Recommended Reading

Berners-Lee, Tim, "Style Guide for Online Hypertext," *http://www. w3.org/pub/WWW/Provider/Style/All.html.*

December, John, and Mark Ginsburg, *HTML and CGI Unleashed* (Indianapolis: Sams.net Publishing, 1995).

Del Galdo, Elisa M, and J. Nielsen, *International User Interfaces* (New York: John Wiley & Sons, Inc., 1996).

DuCharme, Bob, *XML: The Annotated Specification* (Upper Saddle River, N.J.: Prentice-Hall PTR, 1999).

"Elements of Web Design," *CNET Reviews*, 1997, *http://www.cnet. com/Content/Features/Howto/Design/ss1c.html.*

Fernandes, Tony, *Global Interface Design: A Guide to Designing International User Interfaces* (New York: AP Professional, 1995).

Flynn, Peter, *The World Wide Web Handbook: An HTML Guide for Users, Authors and Publishers* (Boston: International Thomas Computer Press, 1995).

Forsythe, Chris, et al., *Human Factors and Web Development*, Mahwah, N.J.: Lawrence Erlbaum Associates, Inc., 1998).

Fortner, Brand, and Theodore E. Meyer, *Number by Colors, A Guide to Using Color to Understand Technical Data* (New York: Springer-Verlag, 1996).

Goldfarb, Charles F., and Paul Prescod, *The XML Handbook,* Upper Saddle River, N.J.: Prentice-Hall PTR, 1998).

Harold, Elliotte Rusty, *XML: Extensible Markup Language* (New York: IDG Books Worldwide, Inc., 1998).

Horn, Robert E., *Developing Procedures, Policies, and Documentation* (Waltham, Maine: Information Mapping, Inc., 1999).

Horton, William, *The Icon Book: Visual Symbols for Computer Systems and Documentation* (New York: John Wiley & Sons, Inc., 1994).

Horton, William, Lee Taylor, Arthur Ignacio, and Nancy Hoft, *The Web Page Design Cookbook* (New York: John Wiley & Sons, Inc., 1996).

Kinkoph, Sherry, Jennifer Fulton, and Katherine Hanley, *Computers: A Visual Encyclopedia* (Indianapolis: Alpha Books, 1994).

Miller, G. A., *"The Magical Number Seven Plus or Minus Two: Some Limits on Our Capacity to Process Information," Psychological Review, 1956.*

Miller, Richard H., Ph.D., *"Web Interface Design: Learning from Our Past,"* 1997, *http://athos.rutgers.edu/~shklar/www4/.*

Morris, Mary E.S., and Randy J. Hinrichs, *Web Page Design: A Different Multimedia,* Upper Saddle River, N.J.: Prentice Hall PTR, 1996).

Neilsen, Jakob, *"International Usability Testing,"* 1997, *http://www.useit.com/papers/international_usetest.html.*

Nielsen, Jakob, *"Be Succinct! (Writing for the Web)," Alertbox,* March, 1997, *http://www.useit.com/alertbox/9703b.html.*

Nielsen, Jakob, *"The Need for Speed," Alertbox,* March, 1997, *http://www.useit.com/alertbox/9703a.html.*

Nielsen, Jakob, *"Why Frames Suck (Most of the Time)," Alertbox,* December, 1996, *http://www.useit.com/alertbox/9612.html.*

Nielsen, Jakob, *"Accessible Design for Users with Disabilities," Alertbox,* October, 1996, *http://www.useit.com/alertbox/9610.html.*

Nielsen, Jakob, *"International Usability," Alertbox,* August, 1996, *http://www.useit.com/alertbox/9608.html.*

Nielsen, Jakob, *"Ten Top Mistakes in Web Design," Alertbox,* May, 1996, *http://www.useit.com/alertbox/9605.html.*

Nielsen, Jakob, 1995, *"Using Paper Prototypes in Home-Page Design,"* IEEE Software, Vol. 12, No.4 (July) 88–89, 97.

Pfaffenberger, Bryan, *World Wide Web Bible* (New York: Henry Holt, 1995).

Pitts-Moultis, Natanya and Cheryl Kirk, *XML Black Book: Indispensable Problem Solver* (Scottsdale: The Coriolis Group, Inc., 1999).

Sano, Darrell, *Designing Large-Scale Web Sites: A Visual Design Methodology* (New York: Wiley Computer Publishing, 1996).

Siegel David, *Creating Killer Web Sites: The Art of Third-Generation Site Design*, 2d ed. (Indianapolis: Hayden Books, 1997).

Siegel, David, *Secrets of Successful Web Sites: Project Management on the World Wide Web* (Indianapolis: Hayden Books, 1999).

Spool, Jared M., et al., *Web Site Usability: A Designer's Guide* (San Francisco: Morgan Kaufmann Publishers, Inc., 1999).

Stross, Charles, *The Web Architect's Handbook* (New York: Addison Wesley, 1996).

"Guide to Web Style," Sun Microsystems, 1997, *http://www.sun. com/styleguide/others/*.

"User Interface Design: Testing Paper Mock-up of Homepage," Sun Microsystems, 1997, *http://www.sun.com/sun-on-net/uidesign/ papertest.html*.

"User Interface Design: Usability Testing of WWW Designs," Sun Microsystems, 1997, *http://www.sun.com/sun-on-net/uidesign/ usabilitytest.html*.

Waters, Crystal, *Web Concept and Design: A Comprehensive Guide for Creating Effective Web Sites* (Indianapolis: New Riders, 1996).

Weinman, Lynda, *Designing Web Graphics: How to Prepare Images and Media for the Web* (Indianapolis: New Riders, 1996).

Weinman, Lynda, *Designing Web Graphics: How to Prepare Images and Media for the Web*, 2d ed. (Indianapolis: New Riders, 1997).

Will-Harris, Daniel, "Adding Graphics to Your Web Pages," CNET Reviews, 1997, *http://www.cnet.com/Content/Features/Howto/ Graphics/*.

B XML Specification

*T*his appendix shows the XML Specification 1.0.

REC-xml-19980210

◆ Extensible Markup Language (XML) 1.0

W3C Recommendation 10 February 1998

This version:
 http://www.w3.org/TR/1998/REC-xml-19980210
 http://www.w3.org/TR/1998/REC-xml-19980210.xml
 http://www.w3.org/TR/1998/REC-xml-19980210.html
 http://www.w3.org/TR/1998/REC-xml-19980210.pdf
 http://www.w3.org/TR/1998/REC-xml-19980210.ps

Latest version:
 http://www.w3.org/TR/REC-xml

Previous version:
 http://www.w3.org/TR/PR-xml-971208

Editors:
 Tim Bray (Textuality and Netscape) *tbray@textuality.com*
 Jean Paoli (Microsoft) *jeanpa@microsoft.com*
 C. M. Sperberg-McQueen (University of Illinois at
  Chicago) *cmsmcq@uic.edu*

◆ Abstract

The Extensible Markup Language (XML) is a subset of SGML that is completely described in this document. Its goal is to enable generic SGML to be served, received, and processed on the Web in the way that is now possible with HTML. XML has been designed for ease of implementation and for interoperability with both SGML and HTML.

◆ Status of this document

This document has been reviewed by W3C Members and other interested parties and has been endorsed by the Director as a W3C Recommendation. It is a stable document and may be used as reference material or cited as a normative reference from another document. W3C's role in making the Recommendation is to draw attention to the specification and to promote its widespread deployment. This enhances the functionality and interoperability of the Web.

This document specifies a syntax created by subsetting an existing, widely used international text processing standard (Standard Generalized Markup Language, ISO 8879:1986(E) as amended and corrected) for use on the World Wide Web. It is a product of the W3C XML Activity, details of which can be found at *http://www.w3.org/XML*. A list of current W3C Recommendations and other technical documents can be found at *http://www.w3.org/TR*.

This specification uses the term URI, which is defined by [*Berners-Lee et al.*], a work in progress expected to update [*IETF RFC1738*] and [*IETF RFC1808*].

The list of known errors in this specification is available at *http://www.w3.org/XML/xml-19980210-errata*.

Please report errors in this document to *xml-editor@w3.org*.

◆ Table of Contents

1. Introduction

Extensible Markup Language, abbreviated XML, describes a class of data objects called *XML documents* and partially describes the behavior of computer programs which process them. XML is an application profile or restricted form of SGML, the Standard Generalized Markup Language [ISO 8879]. By construction, XML documents are conforming SGML documents.

XML documents are made up of storage units called *entities,* which contain either parsed or unparsed data. Parsed data is made up of characters, some of which form character data, and some of which form markup. Markup encodes a description of the document's storage layout and logical structure. XML provides a mechanism to impose constraints on the storage layout and logical structure.

A software module called an **XML processor** is used to read XML documents and provide access to their content and structure. It is assumed that an XML processor is doing its work on behalf of another module, called the **application**. This specification describes the required behavior of an XML processor in terms of how it must read XML data and the information it must provide to the application.

1.1 Origin and Goals

XML was developed by an XML Working Group (originally known as the SGML Editorial Review Board) formed under the auspices of the World Wide Web Consortium (W3C) in 1996. It was chaired by Jon Bosak of Sun Microsystems with the active participation of an XML Special Interest Group (previously known as the SGML Working Group) also organized by the W3C. The membership of the XML Working Group is given in an appendix. Dan Connolly served as the WG's contact with the W3C.

The design goals for XML are:

1. XML shall be straightforwardly usable over the Internet.
2. XML shall support a wide variety of applications.
3. XML shall be compatible with SGML.
4. It shall be easy to write programs which process XML documents.
5. The number of optional features in XML is to be kept to the absolute minimum, ideally zero.
6. XML documents should be human-legible and reasonably clear.
7. The XML design should be prepared quickly.
8. The design of XML shall be formal and concise.
9. XML documents shall be easy to create.
10. Terseness in XML markup is of minimal importance.

This specification, together with associated standards (Unicode and ISO/IEC 10646 for characters, Internet RFC 1766 for language identification tags, ISO 639 for language name codes, and ISO 3166 for country name codes), provides all the information necessary to understand XML Version 1.0 and construct computer programs to process it.

This version of the XML specification may be distributed freely, as long as all text and legal notices remain intact.

1.2 Terminology

The terminology used to describe XML documents is defined in the body of this specification. The terms defined in the following list are used in building those definitions and in describing the actions of an XML processor:

may
Conforming documents and XML processors are permitted to but need not behave as described.

must

Conforming documents and XML processors are required to behave as described; otherwise they are in error.

error

A violation of the rules of this specification; results are undefined. Conforming software may detect and report an error and may recover from it.

fatal error

An error which a conforming XML processor must detect and report to the application. After encountering a fatal error, the processor may continue processing the data to search for further errors and may report such errors to the application. In order to support correction of errors, the processor may make unprocessed data from the document (with intermingled character data and markup) available to the application. Once a fatal error is detected, however, the processor must not continue normal processing (i.e., it must not continue to pass character data and information about the document's logical structure to the application in the normal way).

at user option

Conforming software may or must (depending on the modal verb in the sentence) behave as described; if it does, it must provide users a means to enable or disable the behavior described.

validity constraint

A rule which applies to all valid XML documents. Violations of validity constraints are errors; they must, at user option, be reported by validating XML processors.

well-formedness constraint

A rule which applies to all well-formed XML documents. Violations of well-formedness constraints are fatal errors.

match

(Of strings or names:) Two strings or names being compared must be identical. Characters with multiple possible representations in ISO/IEC 10646 (e.g., characters with both precomposed and base+diacritic forms) match only if they have the same representation in both strings. At user option, processors may normalize such characters to some canonical form. No case folding is performed. (Of strings and rules in the grammar:) A string matches a grammatical production if it belongs to the language generated by that production. (Of content and content models:) An element matches its declaration when it conforms in the fashion described in the constraint "Element Valid".

for compatibility

A feature of XML included solely to ensure that XML remains compatible with SGML.

for interoperability

A non-binding recommendation included to increase the chances that XML documents can be processed by the existing installed base of SGML processors which predate the WebSGML Adaptations Annex to ISO 8879.

2. Documents

A data object is an **XML document** if it is well-formed, as defined in this specification. A well-formed XML document may in addition be valid if it meets certain further constraints.

Each XML document has both a logical and a physical structure. Physically, the document is composed of units called entities. An entity may refer to other entities to cause their inclusion in the document. A document begins in a "root" or document entity. Logically, the document is composed of declarations, elements, comments, character references, and processing instructions, all of which are indicated in the document by explicit markup. The logical and physical structures must nest properly, as described in "4.3.2 Well-Formed Parsed Entities".

2.1 Well-Formed XML Documents

A textual object is a well-formed XML document if:

1. Taken as a whole, it matches the production labeled `document`.
2. It meets all the well-formedness constraints given in this specification.
3. Each of the parsed entities which is referenced directly or indirectly within the document is well-formed.

DOCUMENT

[1] document ::= prolog element Misc*

Matching the `document` production implies that:

1. It contains one or more elements.
2. There is exactly one element, called the **root,** or document element, no part of which appears in the content of any other element. For all other elements, if the start-tag is in the content of another element, the end-tag is in the content of the same element. More simply stated, the

elements, delimited by start- and end-tags, nest properly within each other.

As a consequence of this, for each non-root element C in the document, there is one other element P in the document such that C is in the content of P, but is not in the content of any other element that is in the content of P. P is referred to as the **parent** of C, and C as a **child** of P.

2.2 Characters

A parsed entity contains **text,** a sequence of characters, which may represent markup or character data. A **character** is an atomic unit of text as specified by ISO/IEC 10646 [ISO/IEC 10646]. Legal characters are tab, carriage return, line feed, and the legal graphic characters of Unicode and ISO/IEC 10646. The use of "compatibility characters", as defined in section 6.8 of [Unicode], is discouraged.

CHARACTER RANGE

```
[2] Char ::= #x9      | #xA      | #xD /* any Unicode character,
              | [#x20-#xD7FF]                 excluding the surro-
              | [#xE000-#xFFFD]               gate blocks, FFFE, and
              | [#x10000-#x10FFFF]            FFFF. */
```

The mechanism for encoding character code points into bit patterns may vary from entity to entity. All XML processors must accept the UTF-8 and UTF-16 encodings of 10646; the mechanisms for signaling which of the two is in use, or for bringing other encodings into play, are discussed later, in "4.3.3 Character Encoding in Entities".

2.3 Common Syntactic Constructs

This section defines some symbols used widely in the grammar.

S (white space) consists of one or more space (#x20) characters, carriage returns, line feeds, or tabs.

WHITE SPACE

```
[3] S ::= (#x20 | #x9 | #xD | #xA)+
```

Characters are classified for convenience as letters, digits, or other characters. Letters consist of an alphabetic or syllabic base character possibly followed by one or more combining characters, or of an ideographic character. Full definitions of the specific characters in each class are given in "B. Character Classes".

A **Name** is a token beginning with a letter or one of a few punctuation characters, and continuing with letters, digits, hyphens, underscores, colons, or full stops, together known as name characters. Names beginning with the string "xml", or any string which would match (('X' | 'x') ('M' | 'm') ('L' | 'l')), are reserved for standardization in this or future versions of this specification.

Note: The colon character within XML names is reserved for experimentation with name spaces. Its meaning is expected to be standardized at some future point, at which point those documents using the colon for experimental purposes may need to be updated. (There is no guarantee that any name-space mechanism adopted for XML will in fact use the colon as a name-space delimiter.) In practice, this means that authors should not use the colon in XML names except as part of name-space experiments, but that XML processors should accept the colon as a name character.

An Nmtoken (name token) is any mixture of name characters.

NAMES AND TOKENS

```
[4] NameChar ::= Letter   | Digit  | '.'  | '-'  | '_'  | ':'
                          | CombiningChar | Extender
[5]     Name ::= (Letter | '_' | ':') (NameChar)*
[6]    Names ::= Name (S Name)*
[7]  Nmtoken ::= (NameChar)+
[8] Nmtokens ::= Nmtoken (S Nmtoken)*
```

Literal data is any quoted string not containing the quotation mark used as a delimiter for that string. Literals are used for specifying the content of internal entities (EntityValue), the values of attributes (AttValue), and external identifiers (System Literal). Note that a SystemLiteral can be parsed without scanning for markup.

LITERALS

```
[9]    EntityValue ::= '"' ([^%&"] | PEReference | Reference)*
                       '"'
                   |       "'" ([^%&'] | PEReference
                   | Reference)* "'"
[10]     AttValue ::= '"' ([^<&"] | Reference)* '"'

                   |   "'" ([^<&'] | Reference)* "'"
[11] SystemLiteral ::= ('"' [^"]* '"') | ("'" [^']* "'")
[12] PubidLiteral ::= '"' PubidChar* '"' | "'" (PubidChar -
                       "'")* "'"
[13]    PubidChar ::= #x20 | #xD | #xA | [a-zA-Z0-9] | [-
                       '()+,./:=?;!*#@$_%]
```

2.4 Character Data and Markup

Text consists of intermingled character data and markup. **Markup** takes the form of start-tags, end-tags, empty-element tags, entity references, character references, comments, CDATA section delimiters, document type declarations, and processing instructions.

All text that is not markup constitutes the **character data** of the document.

The ampersand character (&) and the left angle bracket (<) may appear in their literal form only when used as markup delimiters, or within a comment, a processing instruction, or a CDATA section. They are also legal within the literal entity value of an internal entity declaration; see "4.3.2 Well-Formed Parsed Entities". If they are needed elsewhere, they must be escaped using either numeric character references or the strings "&" and "<" respectively. The right angle bracket (>) may be represented using the string ">", and must, for compatibility, be escaped using ">" or a character reference when it appears in the string "]]>" in content, when that string is not marking the end of a CDATA section.

In the content of elements, character data is any string of characters which does not contain the start-delimiter of any markup. In a CDATA section, character data is any string of characters not including the CDATA-section-close delimiter, "]]>".

To allow attribute values to contain both single and double quotes, the apostrophe or single-quote character (') may be represented as "'", and the double-quote character (") as """.

CHARACTER DATA

```
[14] CharData ::= [^<&]* - ([^<&]* ']]>' [^<&]*)
```

2.5 Comments

Comments may appear anywhere in a document outside other markup; in addition, they may appear within the document type declaration at places allowed by the grammar. They are not part of the document's character data; an XML processor may, but need not, make it possible for an application to retrieve the text of comments. For compatibility, the string "--" (double-hyphen) must not occur within comments.

COMMENTS

```
[15] Comment ::= '<!--' ((Char - '-') | ('-' (Char - '-')))
                 '-->'
```

An example of a comment:

```
<!- declarations for <head> & <body> ->
```

2.6 Processing Instructions

Processing instructions (PIs) allow documents to contain instructions for applications.

PROCESSING INSTRUCTIONS

```
[16]       PI ::= '<?' PITarget     (S (Char*  - (Char*   '?>'
                  Char*)))? '?>'
[17] PITarget ::= Name - (('X' | 'x') ('M' | 'm') ('L' | 'l'))
```

PIs are not part of the document's character data, but must be passed through to the application. The PI begins with a target (PITarget) used to identify the application to which the instruction is directed. The target names "XML", "xml", and so on are reserved for standardization in this or future versions of this specification. The XML Notation mechanism may be used for formal declaration of PI targets.

2.7 CDATA Sections

CDATA sections may occur anywhere character data may occur; they are used to escape blocks of text containing characters which would otherwise be recognized as markup. CDATA sections begin with the string "`<![CDATA[`" and end with the string "`]]>`":

CDATA SECTIONS

```
[18]    CDSect  ::= CDStart CData CDEnd
[19]    CDStart ::= '<![CDATA['
[20]     CData  ::= (Char* - (Char* ']]>' Char*))
[21]     CDEnd  ::= ']]>'
```

Within a CDATA section, only the CDEnd string is recognized as markup, so that left angle brackets and ampersands may occur in their literal form; they need not (and cannot) be escaped using "`&lt;`" and "`&amp;`". CDATA sections cannot nest.

An example of a CDATA section, in which "`<greeting>`" and "`</greeting>`" are recognized as character data, not markup:

```
<![CDATA[<greeting>Hello, world!</greeting>]]>
```

2.8 Prolog and Document Type Declaration

XML documents may, and should, begin with an **XML declaration** which specifies the version of XML being used. For example, the following is a complete XML document, well-formed but not valid:

```
<?xml version="1.0"?>
<greeting>Hello, world!</greeting>
```

and so is this:

```
<greeting>Hello, world!</greeting>
```

The version number "1.0" should be used to indicate conformance to this version of this specification; it is an error for a document to use the value "1.0" if it does not conform to this version of this specification. It is the intent of the XML working group to give later versions of this specification number other than "1.0", but this intent does not indicate a commitment to produce any future versions of XML, nor if any are produced, to use any particular numbering scheme. Since future versions are not ruled out, this construct is provided as a means to allow the possibility of automatic version recognition, should it become necessary. Processors may signal an error if they receive documents labeled with versions they do not support.

The function of the markup in an XML document is to describe its storage and logical structure and to associate attribute-value pairs with its logical structures. XML provides a mechanism, the document type declaration, to define constraints on the logical structure and to support the use of predefined storage units. An XML document is **valid** if it has an associated document type declaration and if the document complies with the constraints expressed in it.

The document type declaration must appear before the first element in the document.

PROLOG

```
[22]        prolog ::= XMLDecl? Misc* (doctypedecl Misc*)?
[23]       XMLDecl ::= '<?xml' VersionInfo EncodingDecl? SDDecl?
                       S? '?>'
[24] VersionInfo ::= S 'version' Eq (' VersionNum ' | "
                     VersionNum ")
[25]            Eq ::= S? '=' S?
[26]    VersionNum ::= ([a-zA-Z0-9_.:] | '-')+
[27]          Misc ::= Comment | PI | S
```

The XML **document type declaration** contains or points to markup declarations that provide a grammar for a class of documents. This grammar is known as a document type definition, or **DTD**. The document type declaration can point to an external subset (a special kind of external entity) containing markup declarations, or can contain the markup declarations directly in an internal subset, or can do both. The DTD for a document consists of both subsets taken together.

A **markup declaration** is an element type declaration, an attribute-list declaration, an entity declaration, or a notation declaration. These declarations may be contained in whole or in part within parameter entities, as described in the well-formedness and validity constraints below. For fuller information, see "4. Physical Structures".

DOCUMENT TYPE DEFINITION

```
[28]  doctypedecl ::= '<!DOCTYPE'  S  Name    (S [ VC:       Root
                      ExternalID)?     S?      ('[' Element Type
                      (markupdecl  | PEReference  ]
                      | S)* ']' S?)? '>'
[29]  markupdecl  ::= elementdecl  | AttlistDecl [ VC:     Proper
                      | EntityDecl                        Declara-
                      | NotationDecl      | PI   tion/PE
                      Comment                       Nesting ]
                                              [ WFC: PEs in
                                                Internal
                                                Subset ]
```

The markup declarations may be made up in whole or in part of the replacement text of parameter entities. The productions later in this specification for individual nonterminals (elementdecl, AttlistDecl, and so on) describe the declarations after all the parameter entities have been included.

VALIDITY CONSTRAINT: ROOT ELEMENT TYPE • The Name in the document type declaration must match the element type of the root element.

VALIDITY CONSTRAINT: PROPER DECLARATION/PE NESTING • Parameter-entity replacement text must be properly nested with markup declarations. That is to say, if either the first character or the last character of a markup declaration (markupdecl above) is contained in the replacement text for a parameter-entity reference, both must be contained in the same replacement text.

WELL-FORMEDNESS CONSTRAINT: PEs IN INTERNAL SUBSET • In the internal DTD subset, parameter-entity references can occur only where markup declarations can occur, not within markup declarations. (This does not apply to references that occur in external parameter entities or to the external subset.)

Like the internal subset, the external subset and any external parameter entities referred to in the DTD must consist of a series of complete markup declarations of the types allowed by the non-terminal symbol markupdecl, interspersed with white space or parameter-entity references. However, portions of the contents of the external subset or of external parameter entities may conditionally be ignored by using the conditional section construct; this is not allowed in the internal subset.

EXTERNAL SUBSET

```
[30]     extSubset ::= TextDecl? extSubsetDecl
[31] extSubsetDecl ::= (        markupdecl    | conditionalSect
                       | PEReference | S )*
```

The external subset and external parameter entities also differ from the internal subset in that in them, parameter-entity references are permitted *within* markup declarations, not only *between* markup declarations.

An example of an XML document with a document type declaration:

```
<?xml version="1.0"?>
<!DOCTYPE greeting SYSTEM "hello.dtd">
<greeting>Hello, world!</greeting>
```

The system identifier "hello.dtd" gives the URI of a DTD for the document.

The declarations can also be given locally, as in this example:

```
<?xml version="1.0" encoding="UTF-8" ?>
<!DOCTYPE greeting [
<!ELEMENT greeting (#PCDATA)>
]>
<greeting>Hello, world!</greeting>
```

If both the external and internal subsets are used, the internal subset is considered to occur before the external subset. This has the effect that entity and attribute-list declarations in the internal subset take precedence over those in the external subset.

2.9 Standalone Document Declaration

Markup declarations can affect the content of the document, as passed from an XML processor to an application; examples are attribute defaults and entity declarations. The standalone document declaration, which may appear as a component of the XML declaration, signals whether or not there are such declarations which appear external to the document entity.

STANDALONE DOCUMENT DECLARATION

```
[32] SDDecl ::= S 'standalone' Eq (("'" [ VC: Standalone
              ('yes' | 'no') "'") | ('"' Document  Decla-
              ('yes' | 'no') '"'))      ration ]
```

In a standalone document declaration, the value "yes" indicates that there are no markup declarations external to the document entity (either in the DTD external subset or in an external parameter entity referenced from the internal subset) which affect the information passed from the XML processor to the application. The value "no" indicates that there are or may be such external markup declarations. Note that the standalone document declaration only denotes the presence of external *declarations;* the presence, in a document, of references to external *entities,* when those entities are internally declared, does not change its standalone status.

If there are no external markup declarations, the standalone document declaration has no meaning. If there are external markup declarations but there is no standalone document declaration, the value "no" is assumed.

Any XML document for which standalone="no" holds can be converted algorithmically to a standalone document, which may be desirable for some network delivery applications.

VALIDITY CONSTRAINT: STANDALONE DOCUMENT DECLARATION • The standalone document declaration must have the value "no" if any external markup declarations contain declarations of:

- attributes with default values, if elements to which these attributes apply appear in the document without specifications of values for these attributes, or
- entities (other than amp, lt, gt, apos, quot), if references to those entities appear in the document, or
- attributes with values subject to normalization, where the attribute appears in the document with a value which will change as a result of normalization, or
- element types with element content, if white space occurs directly within any instance of those types.

An example XML declaration with a standalone document declaration:

```
<?xml version="1.0" standalone='yes'?>
```

2.10 White Space Handling

In editing XML documents, it is often convenient to use "white space" (spaces, tabs, and blank lines, denoted by the nonterminal S in this specification) to set apart the markup for greater readability. Such white space is typically not intended for inclusion in the delivered version of the document. On the other hand, "significant" white space that should be preserved in the delivered version is common, for example in poetry and source code.

An XML processor must always pass all characters in a document that are not markup through to the application. A validating XML processor must also inform the application which of these characters constitute white space appearing in element content.

A special attribute named xml:space may be attached to an element to signal an intention that in that element, white space should be preserved by applications. In valid documents, this attribute, like any other, must be declared if it is used. When declared, it must be given as an enumerated type whose only possible values are "default" and "preserve". For example:

```
<!ATTLIST poem xml:space (default|preserve) 'preserve'>
```

The value "default" signals that applications' default white-space processing modes are acceptable for this element; the value "preserve" indicates the intent that applications preserve all the white space. This declared intent is considered to apply to all elements within the content of the element where it is specified, unless overriden with another instance of the xml:space attribute.

The root element of any document is considered to have signaled no intentions as regards application space handling, unless it provides a value for this attribute or the attribute is declared with a default value.

2.11 End-of-Line Handling

XML parsed entities are often stored in computer files which, for editing convenience, are organized into lines. These lines are typically separated by some combination of the characters carriage-return (#xD) and line-feed (#xA).

To simplify the tasks of applications, wherever an external parsed entity or the literal entity value of an internal parsed entity contains either the literal two-character sequence "#xD#xA" or a standalone literal #xD, an XML processor must pass to the application the single character #xA. (This behavior can conveniently be produced by normalizing all line breaks to #xA on input, before parsing.)

2.12 Language Identification

In document processing, it is often useful to identify the natural or formal language in which the content is written. A special attribute named xml:lang may be inserted in documents to specify the language used in the contents and attribute values of any element in an XML document. In valid documents, this attribute, like any other, must be declared if it is used. The values of the attribute are language identifiers as defined by [IETF RFC 1766], "Tags for the Identification of Languages":

LANGUAGE IDENTIFICATION

```
[33] LanguageID ::= Langcode ('-' Subcode)*
[34]   Langcode ::= ISO639Code | IanaCode | UserCode
[35] ISO639Code ::= ([a-z] | [A-Z]) ([a-z] | [A-Z])
[36]   IanaCode ::= ('i' | 'I') '-' ([a-z] | [A-Z])+
[37]   UserCode ::= ('x' | 'X') '-' ([a-z] | [A-Z])+
[38]   Subcode  ::= ([a-z] | [A-Z])+
```

The Langcode may be any of the following:

- a two-letter language code as defined by [ISO 639], "Codes for the representation of names of languages"
- a language identifier registered with the Internet Assigned Numbers Authority [IANA]; these begin with the prefix "i-" (or "I-")
- a language identifier assigned by the user, or agreed on between parties in private use; these must begin with the

prefix "x-" or "X-" in order to ensure that they do not conflict with names later standardized or registered with IANA

There may be any number of Subcode segments; if the first subcode segment exists and the subcode consists of two letters, then it must be a country code from [ISO 3166], "Codes for the representation of names of countries." If the first subcode consists of more than two letters, it must be a subcode for the language in question registered with IANA, unless the Langcode begins with the prefix "x-" or "X-".

It is customary to give the language code in lower case, and the country code (if any) in upper case. Note that these values, unlike other names in XML documents, are case insensitive.

For example:

```
<p xml:lang="en">The quick brown fox jumps over the lazy dog.</p>
<p xml:lang="en-GB">What colour is it?</p>
<p xml:lang="en-US">What color is it?</p>
<sp who="Faust" desc='leise' xml:lang="de">
<l>Habe nun, ach! Philosophie,</l>
<l>Juristerei, und Medizin</l>
<l>und leider auch Theologie</l>
<l>durchaus studiert mit heißem Bemüh'n.</l>
</sp>
```

The intent declared with xml:lang is considered to apply to all attributes and content of the element where it is specified, unless overridden with an instance of xml:lang on another element within that content.

A simple declaration for xml:lang might take the form

```
xml:lang NMTOKEN #IMPLIED
```

but specific default values may also be given, if appropriate. In a collection of French poems for English students, with glosses and notes in English, the xml:lang attribute might be declared this way:

```
<!ATTLIST poem xml:lang NMTOKEN 'fr'>
<!ATTLIST gloss xml:lang NMTOKEN 'en'>
<!ATTLIST note xml:lang NMTOKEN 'en'>
```

3. Logical Structures

Each XML document contains one or more **elements**, the boundaries of which are either delimited by start-tags and end-tags, or, for empty elements, by an empty-element tag. Each element has a type, identified by name, sometimes called its "generic identifier" (GI), and may have a set of attribute specifications. Each attribute specification has a name and a value.

ELEMENT

```
[39] element ::= EmptyElemTag
                 | STag        content [ WFC: Element Type Match
                 ETag                  ]
                                       [ VC: Element Valid ]
```

This specification does not constrain the semantics, use, or (beyond syntax) names of the element types and attributes, except that names beginning with a match to (('X'|'x') ('M'|'m')('L'|'l')) are reserved for standardization in this or future versions of this specification.

WELL-FORMEDNESS CONSTRAINT: ELEMENT TYPE MATCH • The Name in an element's end-tag must match the element type in the start-tag.

VALIDITY CONSTRAINT: ELEMENT VALID • An element is valid if there is a declaration matching elementdecl where the Name matches the element type, and one of the following holds:

1. The declaration matches EMPTY and the element has no content.
2. The declaration matches children and the sequence of child elements belongs to the language generated by the regular expression in the content model, with optional white space (characters matching the nonterminal S) between each pair of child elements.
3. The declaration matches Mixed and the content consists of character data and child elements whose types match names in the content model.
4. The declaration matches ANY, and the types of any child elements have been declared.

3.1 Start-Tags, End-Tags, and Empty-Element Tags

The beginning of every non-empty XML element is marked by a **start-tag**.

START-TAG

```
[40]    STag ::= '<' Name          (S [ WFC: Unique Att Spec
                 Attribute)* S? '>'   ]
[41] Attribute ::= Name Eq AttValue   [ VC:  Attribute Value
                                        Type ]
                                      [ WFC: No External En-
                                        tity References ]
                                      [ WFC: No < in Attrib-
                                        ute Values ]
```

The `Name` in the start- and end-tags gives the element's **type**. The `NameAttValue` pairs are referred to as the **attribute specifications** of the element, with the `Name` in each pair referred to as the **attribute name** and the content of the `AttValue` (the text between the ' or " delimiters) as the **attribute value**.

WELL-FORMEDNESS CONSTRAINT: UNIQUE ATT SPEC • No attribute name may appear more than once in the same start-tag or empty-element tag.

VALIDITY CONSTRAINT: ATTRIBUTE VALUE TYPE • The attribute must have been declared; the value must be of the type declared for it. (For attribute types, see "3.3 Attribute-List Declarations".)

WELL-FORMEDNESS CONSTRAINT: NO EXTERNAL ENTITY REFERENCES • Attribute values cannot contain direct or indirect entity references to external entities.

WELL-FORMEDNESS CONSTRAINT: NO < IN ATTRIBUTE VALUES • The replacement text of any entity referred to directly or indirectly in an attribute value (other than "<") must not contain a <.

An example of a start-tag:

```
<termdef id="dt-dog" term="dog">
```

The end of every element that begins with a start-tag must be marked by an **end-tag** containing a name that echoes the element's type as given in the start-tag:

END-TAG
```
[42] Etag ::= '</' Name S? '>'
```

An example of an end-tag:

```
</termdef>
```

The text between the start-tag and end-tag is called the element's **content**:

CONTENT OF ELEMENTS
```
[43] content ::= (element | CharData | Reference | CDSect | PI
                 | Comment)*
```

If an element is **empty**, it must be represented either by a start-tag immediately followed by an end-tag or by an empty-element tag. An **empty-element tag** takes a special form:

TAGS FOR EMPTY ELEMENTS
```
[44] EmptyElemTag ::= '<'      Name      (S [ WFC: Unique Att
                            Attribute)* S? '/>'    Spec ]
```

Empty-element tags may be used for any element which has no content, whether or not it is declared using the keyword EMPTY. For interoperability, the empty-element tag must be used, and can only be used, for elements which are declared EMPTY.

Examples of empty elements:

```
<IMG align="left"
 src="http://www.w3.org/Icons/WWW/w3c_home" />
<br></br>
<br/>
```

3.2 Element Type Declarations

The element structure of an XML document may, for validation purposes, be constrained using element type and attribute-list declarations. An element type declaration constrains the element's content.

Element type declarations often constrain which element types can appear as children of the element. At user option, an XML processor may issue a warning when a declaration mentions an element type for which no declaration is provided, but this is not an error.

An **element type declaration** takes the form:

Element Type Declaration

```
[45] elementdecl ::= '<!ELEMENT'  S Name [ VC: Unique Element
                     S   contentspec  S?   Type Declaration ]
                     '>'
[46] contentspec ::= 'EMPTY'       | 'ANY'
                     | Mixed | children
```

---

where the Name gives the element type being declared.

Validity Constraint: Unique Element Type Declaration •
No element type may be declared more than once.

Examples of element type declarations:

```
<!ELEMENT br EMPTY>
<!ELEMENT p (#PCDATA|emph)* >
<!ELEMENT %name.para; %content.para; >
<!ELEMENT container ANY>
```

3.2.1 ELEMENT CONTENT

An element type has **element content** when elements of that type must contain only child elements (no character data), optionally separated by white space (characters matching the nonterminal S). In this case, the constraint includes a content model, a simple grammar governing the allowed types of the child elements and the order in which they are allowed to appear. The grammar is built on content particles (cps), which consist of names, choice lists of content particles, or sequence lists of content particles:

ELEMENT-CONTENT MODELS

```
[47] children ::= (choice   | seq)      ('?'
                   | '*'  | '+')?
[48]      cp ::= (Name   | choice   | seq)
                 ('?'  |  '*'  | '+')?
[49]  choice ::= '('   S? cp ( S?  '|' S? [ VC:           Proper
                 cp )* S? ')'                  Group/PE Nesting ]
[50]     seq ::= '('   S? cp ( S?  ',' S? [ VC:           Proper
                 cp )* S? ')'                  Group/PE Nesting ]
```

where each Name is the type of an element which may appear as a child. Any content particle in a choice list may appear in the element content at the location where the choice list appears in the grammar; content particles occurring in a sequence list must each appear in the element content in the order given in the list. The optional character following a name or list governs whether the element or the content particles in the list may occur one or more (+), zero or more (*), or zero or one times (?). The absence of such an operator means that the element or content particle must appear exactly once. This syntax and meaning are identical to those used in the productions in this specification.

The content of an element matches a content model if and only if it is possible to trace out a path through the content model, obeying the sequence, choice, and repetition operators and matching each element in the content against an element type in the content model. For compatibility, it is an error if an element in the document can match more than one occurrence of an element type in the content model. For more information, see "E. Deterministic Content Models".

VALIDITY CONSTRAINT: PROPER GROUP/PE NESTING • Parameter-entity replacement text must be properly nested with parenthetized groups. That is to say, if either of the opening or closing parentheses in a choice, seq, or Mixed construct is contained in the replacement text for a parameter entity, both must be contained in the same replacement text. For interoperability, if a parameter-entity reference appears in a choice, seq, or Mixed construct, its replacement text should not be empty, and neither the first nor last non-blank character of the replacement text should be a connector (| or ,).

Examples of element-content models:

```
<!ELEMENT spec (front, body, back?)>
<!ELEMENT div1 (head, (p | list | note)*, div2*)>
<!ELEMENT dictionary-body (%div.mix; | %dict.mix;)*>
```

3.2.2 MIXED CONTENT

An element type has **mixed content** when elements of that type may contain character data, optionally interspersed with child elements. In this case, the types of the child elements may be constrained, but not their order or their number of occurrences:

MIXED-CONTENT DECLARATION

```
[51] Mixed ::= '(' S? '#PCDATA' (S?  '|'
                S? Name)* S? ')*'
             | '(' S? '#PCDATA' S? ')'   [ VC: Proper Group/PE
                                           Nesting ]
                                         [ VC:  No  Duplicate
                                           Types ]
```

where the Names give the types of elements that may appear as children.

VALIDITY CONSTRAINT: NO DUPLICATE TYPES • The same name must not appear more than once in a single mixed-content declaration.

Examples of mixed content declarations:

```
<!ELEMENT p (#PCDATA|a|ul|b|i|em)*>
<!ELEMENT p (#PCDATA | %font; | %phrase; | %special; | %form;)* >
<!ELEMENT b (#PCDATA)>
```

3.3 Attribute-List Declarations

Attributes are used to associate name-value pairs with elements. Attribute specifications may appear only within start-tags and empty-element tags; thus, the productions used to recognize them appear in "3.1 Start-Tags, End-Tags, and Empty-Element Tags". Attribute-list declarations may be used:

- To define the set of attributes pertaining to a given element type.

- To establish type constraints for these attributes.
- To provide default values for attributes.

Attribute-list declarations specify the name, data type, and default value (if any) of each attribute associated with a given element type:

ATTRIBUTE-LIST DECLARATION

```
[52] AttlistDecl ::= '<!ATTLIST' S Name AttDef* S? '>'
[53]      AttDef ::= S Name S AttType S DefaultDecl
```

The `Name` in the `AttlistDecl` rule is the type of an element. At user option, an XML processor may issue a warning if attributes are declared for an element type not itself declared, but this is not an error. The `Name` in the `AttDef` rule is the name of the attribute.

When more than one `AttlistDecl` is provided for a given element type, the contents of all those provided are merged. When more than one definition is provided for the same attribute of a given element type, the first declaration is binding and later declarations are ignored. For interoperability, writers of DTDs may choose to provide at most one attribute-list declaration for a given element type, at most one attribute definition for a given attribute name, and at least one attribute definition in each attribute-list declaration. For interoperability, an XML processor may at user option issue a warning when more than one attribute-list declaration is provided for a given element type, or more than one attribute definition is provided for a given attribute, but this is not an error.

3.3.1 ATTRIBUTE TYPES

XML attribute types are of three kinds: a string type, a set of tokenized types, and enumerated types. The string type may take any literal string as a value; the tokenized types have varying lexical and semantic constraints, as noted:

ATTRIBUTE TYPES

```
[54]       AttType ::= StringType
                     | TokenizedType
                     | EnumeratedType
[55]     StringType ::= 'CDATA'
[56] TokenizedType ::= 'ID'              [ VC: ID ]
```

		[VC: One ID per Element Type]
		[VC: ID Attribute Default]
|	'IDREF'	[VC: IDREF]
|	'IDREFS'	[VC: IDREF]
|	'ENTITY'	[VC: Entity Name]
|	'ENTITIES'	[VC: Entity Name]
|	'NMTOKEN'	[VC: Name Token]
|	'NMTOKENS'	[VC: Name Token]

VALIDITY CONSTRAINT: **ID** • Values of type ID must match the Name production. A name must not appear more than once in an XML document as a value of this type; i.e., ID values must uniquely identify the elements which bear them.

VALIDITY CONSTRAINT: ONE **ID** PER ELEMENT TYPE • No element type may have more than one ID attribute specified.

VALIDITY CONSTRAINT: **ID** ATTRIBUTE DEFAULT • An ID attribute must have a declared default of #IMPLIED or #REQUIRED.

VALIDITY CONSTRAINT: **IDREF** • Values of type IDREF must match the Name production, and values of type IDREFS must match Names; each Name must match the value of an ID attribute on some element in the XML document; i.e., IDREF values must match the value of some ID attribute.

VALIDITY CONSTRAINT: ENTITY NAME • Values of type ENTITY must match the Name production, values of type ENTITIES must match Names; each Name must match the name of an unparsed entity declared in the DTD.

VALIDITY CONSTRAINT: NAME TOKEN • Values of type NMTOKEN must match the Nmtoken production; values of type NMTOKENS must match Nmtokens.

Enumerated attributes can take one of a list of values provided in the declaration. There are two kinds of enumerated types:

ENUMERATED ATTRIBUTE TYPES

```
[57]  EnumeratedType  ::= NotationType
                       |  Enumeration
[58]    NotationType  ::= 'NOTATION'   S  '('  S?  [ VC:      Notation
                         Name    (S?    '|'   S?   Attributes ]
                         Name)* S? ')'
[59]     Enumeration  ::= '('   S?   Nmtoken  (S?  [ VC:
                         '|'   S?  Nmtoken)*  S?   Enumeration ]
                         ')'
```

A NOTATION attribute identifies a notation, declared in the DTD with associated system and/or public identifiers, to be used in interpreting the element to which the attribute is attached.

VALIDITY CONSTRAINT: NOTATION ATTRIBUTES • Values of this type must match one of the notation names included in the declaration; all notation names in the declaration must be declared.

VALIDITY CONSTRAINT: ENUMERATION • Values of this type must match one of the Nmtoken tokens in the declaration.

For interoperability, the same Nmtoken should not occur more than once in the enumerated attribute types of a single element type.

3.3.2 ATTRIBUTE DEFAULTS

An attribute declaration provides information on whether the attribute's presence is required, and if not, how an XML processor should react if a declared attribute is absent in a document.

ATTRIBUTE DEFAULTS

```
[60] DefaultDecl ::= '#REQUIRED'
                  |  '#IMPLIED'
                  |  (('#FIXED'    S)? [ VC:    Required    At-
                     AttValue)            tribute ]
                                       [ VC:    Attribute   De-
                                         fault Legal ]
                                       [ WFC:   No  <  in  At-
                                         tribute Values ]
                                       [ VC:    Fixed Attribute
                                         Default ]
```

In an attribute declaration, #REQUIRED means that the attribute must always be provided, #IMPLIED that no default value is provided. If the declaration is neither #REQUIRED nor #IMPLIED, then the AttValue value contains the declared **default** value; the #FIXED keyword states that the attribute must always have the default value. If a default value is declared, when an XML processor encounters an omitted attribute, it is to behave as though the attribute were present with the declared default value.

VALIDITY CONSTRAINT: REQUIRED ATTRIBUTE • If the default declaration is the keyword #REQUIRED, then the attribute must be specified for all elements of the type in the attribute-list declaration.

VALIDITY CONSTRAINT: ATTRIBUTE DEFAULT LEGAL • The declared default value must meet the lexical constraints of the declared attribute type.

VALIDITY CONSTRAINT: FIXED ATTRIBUTE DEFAULT • If an attribute has a default value declared with the #FIXED keyword, instances of that attribute must match the default value.

Examples of attribute-list declarations:

```
<!ATTLIST termdef
          id       ID      #REQUIRED
          name     CDATA   #IMPLIED>
<!ATTLIST list
          type     (bullets|ordered|glossary) "ordered">
<!ATTLIST form
          method   CDATA   #FIXED "POST">
```

3.3.3 ATTRIBUTE-VALUE NORMALIZATION

Before the value of an attribute is passed to the application or checked for validity, the XML processor must normalize it as follows:

- a character reference is processed by appending the referenced character to the attribute value
- an entity reference is processed by recursively processing the replacement text of the entity
- a whitespace character (#x20, #xD, #xA, #x9) is processed by appending #x20 to the normalized value, except that

only a single #x20 is appended for a "#xD#xA" sequence that is part of an external parsed entity or the literal entity value of an internal parsed entity

- other characters are processed by appending them to the normalized value

If the declared value is not CDATA, then the XML processor must further process the normalized attribute value by discarding any leading and trailing space (#x20) characters, and by replacing sequences of space (#x20) characters by a single space (#x20) character.

All attributes for which no declaration has been read should be treated by a non-validating parser as if declared CDATA.

3.4 Conditional Sections

Conditional sections are portions of the document type declaration external subset which are included in, or excluded from, the logical structure of the DTD based on the keyword which governs them.

CONDITIONAL SECTION

```
[61]      conditionalSect ::= includeSect | ignoreSect
[62]         includeSect ::= '<!['    S?    'INCLUDE'    S?    '['
                              extSubsetDecl ']]>'
[63]          ignoreSect ::= '<!['    S?    'IGNORE'    S?    '['
                              ignoreSectContents* ']]>'
[64] ignoreSectContents ::= Ignore    ('<![' ignoreSectContents
                              ']]>' Ignore)*
[65]              Ignore ::= Char*  -  (Char*    ('<![' | ']]>')
                              Char*)
```

Like the internal and external DTD subsets, a conditional section may contain one or more complete declarations, comments, processing instructions, or nested conditional sections, intermingled with white space.

If the keyword of the conditional section is INCLUDE, then the contents of the conditional section are part of the DTD. If the keyword of the conditional section is IGNORE, then the contents of the conditional section are not logically part of the DTD. Note that for reliable parsing, the contents of even ignored conditional sections must be read in order to detect nested conditional sections and ensure that the end of the outermost (ignored) conditional section is properly detected. If a conditional section with a keyword of INCLUDE occurs within a larger conditional section with a keyword of IGNORE, both the outer and the inner conditional sections are ignored.

If the keyword of the conditional section is a parameter-entity reference, the parameter entity must be replaced by its content before the processor decides whether to include or ignore the conditional section.

An example:

```
<!ENTITY % draft 'INCLUDE' >
<!ENTITY % final 'IGNORE' >
<![%draft;[
<!ELEMENT book (comments*, title, body, supplements?)>
]]>
<![%final;[
<!ELEMENT book (title, body, supplements?)>
]]>
```

4. Physical Structures

An XML document may consist of one or many storage units. These are called **entities**; they all have **content** and are all (except for the document entity, see below, and the external DTD subset) identified by **name**. Each XML document has one entity called the document entity, which serves as the starting point for the XML processor and may contain the whole document.

Entities may be either parsed or unparsed. A **parsed entity's** contents are referred to as its replacement text; this text is considered an integral part of the document.

An **unparsed entity** is a resource whose contents may or may not be text, and if text, may not be XML. Each unparsed entity has an associated notation, identified by name. Beyond a requirement that an XML processor make the identifiers for the entity and notation available to the application, XML places no constraints on the contents of unparsed entities.

Parsed entities are invoked by name using entity references; unparsed entities by name, given in the value of ENTITY or EN-TITIES attributes.

General entities are entities for use within the document content. In this specification, general entities are sometimes referred to with the unqualified term *entity* when this leads to no ambiguity. Parameter entities are parsed entities for use within the DTD. These two types of entities use different forms of reference and are recognized in different contexts. Furthermore, they occupy different namespaces; a parameter entity and a general entity with the same name are two distinct entities.

4.1 Character and Entity References

A **character reference** refers to a specific character in the ISO/IEC 10646 character set, for example one not directly accessible from available input devices.

CHARACTER REFERENCE
```
[66] CharRef ::= '&#' [0-9]+ ';'
                | '&#x'  [0-9a-fA-F]+ [WFC: Legal Character
                ';'                  ]
```

WELL-FORMEDNESS CONSTRAINT: LEGAL CHARACTER • Characters referred to using character references must match the production for Char.

If the character reference begins with "&#x", the digits and letters up to the terminating ; provide a hexadecimal representation of the character's code point in ISO/IEC 10646. If it begins just with "&#", the digits up to the terminating ; provide a decimal representation of the character's code point.

An **entity reference** refers to the content of a named entity. References to parsed general entities use ampersand (&) and semicolon (;) as delimiters. **Parameter-entity references** use percent-sign (%) and semicolon (;) as delimiters.

ENTITY REFERENCE
```
[67]   Reference ::= EntityRef
                    | CharRef
[68]   EntityRef ::= '&' Name ';'       [ WFC: Entity Declared
                                        ]
                                        [ VC:  Entity Declared
                                        ]
                                        [ WFC: Parsed Entity ]
                                        [ WFC: No Recursion ]
[69] PEReference ::= '%' Name ';'       [ VC:  Entity Declared
                                        ]
                                        [ WFC: No Recursion ]
                                        [ WFC: In DTD ]
```

WELL-FORMEDNESS CONSTRAINT: ENTITY DECLARED • In a document without any DTD, a document with only an internal DTD subset which contains no parameter entity references, or a document with "standalone='yes'", the Name given in the entity reference must match that in an entity declaration, except that well-formed documents need not declare any of the following entities: amp, lt, gt, apos, quot. The declaration of a parameter entity must precede any reference to it. Similarly, the declaration of a general entity must precede any reference to it which appears in a default value in an attribute-list declaration. Note that if entities are declared in the external subset or in external parameter entities, a non-validating processor is not obligated to read and process their declarations; for such documents, the rule that an entity must be declared is a well-formedness constraint only if standalone='yes'.

VALIDITY CONSTRAINT: ENTITY DECLARED • In a document with an external subset or external parameter entities with "standalone='no'", the Name given in the entity reference must match that in an entity declaration. For interoperability, valid documents should declare the entities amp, lt, gt, apos, quot, in the form specified in "4.6 Predefined Entities". The declaration of a parameter entity must precede any reference to it. Similarly, the declaration of a general entity must precede any reference to it which appears in a default value in an attribute-list declaration.

WELL-FORMEDNESS CONSTRAINT: PARSED ENTITY • An entity reference must not contain the name of an unparsed entity. Unparsed entities may be referred to only in attribute values declared to be of type ENTITY or ENTITIES.

WELL-FORMEDNESS CONSTRAINT: NO RECURSION • A parsed entity must not contain a recursive reference to itself, either directly or indirectly.

WELL-FORMEDNESS CONSTRAINT: IN DTD • Parameter-entity references may only appear in the DTD.
Examples of character and entity references:

```
Type <key>less-than</key> (&#x3C;) to save options.
This document was prepared on &docdate; and
is classified &security-level; .
```

Example of a parameter-entity reference:

```
<!— declare the parameter entity "ISOLat2"... —>
<!ENTITY % ISOLat2
        SYSTEM "http://www.xml.com/iso/isolat2-
xml.entities" >
<!— ... now reference it. —>
%ISOLat2;
```

4.2 Entity Declarations

Entities are declared thus:

ENTITY DECLARATION
```
[70] EntityDecl ::= GEDecl | PEDecl
[71]     GEDecl ::= '<!ENTITY' S Name S EntityDef S? '>'
[72]     PEDecl ::= '<!ENTITY' S '%' S Name S PEDef S? '>'
[73] EntityDef ::= EntityValue | (ExternalID NDataDecl?)
[74]     PEDef ::= EntityValue | ExternalID
```

The `Name` identifies the entity in an entity reference or, in the case of an unparsed entity, in the value of an `ENTITY` or `ENTITIES` attribute. If the same entity is declared more than once, the first declaration encountered is binding; at user option, an XML processor may issue a warning if entities are declared multiple times.

4.2.1 INTERNAL ENTITIES

If the entity definition is an `EntityValue`, the defined entity is called an **internal entity**. There is no separate physical storage object, and the content of the entity is given in the declaration. Note that some processing of entity and character references in the literal entity value may be required to produce the correct replacement text: see "4.5 Construction of Internal Entity Replacement Text".

An internal entity is a parsed entity.

Example of an internal entity declaration:

```
<!ENTITY Pub-Status "This is a pre-release of the
  specification.">
```

4.2.2 EXTERNAL ENTITIES

If the entity is not internal, it is an **external entity**, declared as follows:

EXTERNAL ENTITY DECLARATION

```
[75] ExternalID ::= 'SYSTEM' S SystemLiteral
               | 'PUBLIC' S PubidLiteral
                 S SystemLiteral
[76] NdataDecl ::= S 'NDATA' S Name          [ VC:    Notation
                                               Declared ]
```

If the `NDataDecl` is present, this is a general unparsed entity; otherwise it is a parsed entity.

VALIDITY CONSTRAINT: NOTATION DECLARED • The `Name` must match the declared name of a notation.

The `SystemLiteral` is called the entity's **system identifier**. It is a URI, which may be used to retrieve the entity. Note that the hash mark (#) and fragment identifier frequently used with URIs are not, formally, part of the URI itself; an XML processor may signal an error if a fragment identifier is given as part of a system identifier. Unless otherwise provided by information outside the scope of this specification (e.g. a special XML element type defined by a particular DTD, or a processing instruction defined by a particular application specification), relative URIs are relative to the location of the resource within which the entity declaration occurs. A URI might thus be relative to the document entity, to the entity containing the external DTD subset, or to some other external parameter entity.

An XML processor should handle a non-ASCII character in a URI by representing the character in UTF-8 as one or more bytes, and then escaping these bytes with the URI escaping mechanism (i.e., by converting each byte to %HH, where HH is the hexadecimal notation of the byte value).

In addition to a system identifier, an external identifier may include a **public identifier**. An XML processor attempting to retrieve the entity's content may use the public identifier to try to generate an alternative URI. If the processor is unable to do so, it must use the URI specified in the system literal. Before a match is attempted, all strings of white space in the public identifier must be normalized to single space characters (#x20), and leading and trailing white space must be removed.

Examples of external entity declarations:

```
<!ENTITY open-hatch
        SYSTEM "http://www.textuality.com/boilerplate/Open-
Hatch.xml">
<!ENTITY open-hatch
        PUBLIC "-//Textuality//TEXT Standard open-
hatch boilerplate//EN"
        "http://www.textuality.com/boilerplate/OpenHatch.xml">
<!ENTITY hatch-pic
        SYSTEM "../grafix/OpenHatch.gif"
        NDATA gif >
```

4.3 Parsed Entities

4.3.1 THE TEXT DECLARATION

External parsed entities may each begin with a **text declaration**.

TEXT DECLARATION
```
[77] TextDecl ::= '<?xml' VersionInfo? EncodingDecl S? '?>'
```

The text declaration must be provided literally, not by reference to a parsed entity. No text declaration may appear at any position other than the beginning of an external parsed entity.

4.3.2 WELL-FORMED PARSED ENTITIES

The document entity is well-formed if it matches the production labeled document. An external general parsed entity is well-formed if it matches the production labeled extParsedEnt. An external parameter entity is well-formed if it matches the production labeled extPE.

WELL-FORMED EXTERNAL PARSED ENTITY
```
[78] extParsedEnt ::= TextDecl? content
[79]       extPE ::= TextDecl? extSubsetDecl
```

An internal general parsed entity is well-formed if its replacement text matches the production labeled content. All internal parameter entities are well-formed by definition.

A consequence of well-formedness in entities is that the logical and physical structures in an XML document are properly nested; no start-tag, end-tag, empty-element tag, element, comment, processing instruction, character reference, or entity reference can begin in one entity and end in another.

4.3.3 CHARACTER ENCODING IN ENTITIES

Each external parsed entity in an XML document may use a different encoding for its characters. All XML processors must be able to read entities in either UTF-8 or UTF-16.

Entities encoded in UTF-16 must begin with the Byte Order Mark described by ISO/IEC 10646 Annex E and Unicode Appendix B (the ZERO WIDTH NO-BREAK SPACE character, #xFEFF). This is an encoding signature, not part of either the markup or the character data of the XML document. XML processors must be able to use this character to differentiate between UTF-8 and UTF-16 encoded documents.

Although an XML processor is required to read only entities in the UTF-8 and UTF-16 encodings, it is recognized that other encodings are used around the world, and it may be desired for XML processors to read entities that use them. Parsed entities which are stored in an encoding other than UTF-8 or UTF-16 must begin with a text declaration containing an encoding declaration:

ENCODING DECLARATION

```
[80] EncodingDecl ::= S 'encoding'  Eq
                      ('"'  EncName  '"'
                      |  "'" EncName  "'"
                      )
[81]      EncName ::= [A-Za-z] ([A-Za-z0-/* Encoding   name
                      9._] | '-')*          contains   only
                                            Latin characters
                                            */
```

In the document entity, the encoding declaration is part of the XML declaration. The EncName is the name of the encoding used.

In an encoding declaration, the values "UTF-8", "UTF-16", "ISO-10646-UCS-2", and "ISO-10646-UCS-4" should be used for the various encodings and transformations of Unicode / ISO/IEC 10646, the values "ISO-8859-1", "ISO-8859-2",...

"ISO-8859-9" should be used for the parts of ISO 8859, and the values "ISO-2022-JP", "Shift_JIS", and "EUC-JP" should be used for the various encoded forms of JIS X-0208-1997. XML processors may recognize other encodings; it is recommended that character encodings registered (as *charsets*) with the Internet Assigned Numbers Authority [IANA], other than those just listed, should be referred to using their registered names. Note that these registered names are defined to be case-insensitive, so processors wishing to match against them should do so in a case-insensitive way.

In the absence of information provided by an external transport protocol (e.g., HTTP or MIME), it is an error for an entity including an encoding declaration to be presented to the XML processor in an encoding other than that named in the declaration, for an encoding declaration to occur other than at the beginning of an external entity, or for an entity which begins with neither a Byte Order Mark nor an encoding declaration to use an encoding other than UTF-8. Note that since ASCII is a subset of UTF-8, ordinary ASCII entities do not strictly need an encoding declaration.

It is a fatal error when an XML processor encounters an entity with an encoding that it is unable to process.

Examples of encoding declarations:

```
<?xml encoding='UTF-8'?>
<?xml encoding='EUC-JP'?>
```

4.4 XML Processor Treatment of Entities and References

The table below summarizes the contexts in which character references, entity references, and invocations of unparsed entities might appear and the required behavior of an XML processor in each case. The labels in the leftmost column describe the recognition context:

Reference in Content

as a reference anywhere after the start-tag and before the end-tag of an element; corresponds to the nonterminal content.

Reference in Attribute Value

as a reference within either the value of an attribute in a start-tag, or a default value in an attribute declaration; corresponds to the nonterminal AttValue.

Occurs as Attribute Value

as a Name, not a reference, appearing either as the value of an attribute which has been declared as type ENTITY, or as one of the space-separated tokens in the value of an attribute which has been declared as type ENTITIES.

Reference in Entity Value

as a reference within a parameter or internal entity's literal entity value in the entity's declaration; corresponds to the nonterminal Entity-Value.

Reference in DTD

as a reference within either the internal or external subsets of the DTD, but outside of an EntityValue or AttValue.

	Entity Type				
	Parameter	**Internal General**	**External Parsed General**	**Unparsed**	**Character**
Reference in Content	Not recognized	Included	Included if validating	Forbidden	Included
Reference in Attribute Value	Not recognized	Included in literal	Forbidden	Forbidden	Included
Occurs as Attribute Value	Not recognized	Forbidden	Forbidden	Notify	Not recognized
Reference in EntityValue	Included in literal	Bypassed	Bypassed	Forbidden	Included
Reference in DTD	Included as PE	Forbidden	Forbidden	Forbidden	Forbidden

4.4.1 NOT RECOGNIZED

Outside the DTD, the % character has no special significance; thus, what would be parameter entity references in the DTD are not recognized as markup in content. Similarly, the names of unparsed entities are not recognized except when they appear in the value of an appropriately declared attribute.

4.4.2 INCLUDED

An entity is **included** when its replacement text is retrieved and processed, in place of the reference itself, as though it were part of the document at the location the reference was recognized. The replacement text may contain both character data and (except for parameter entities) markup, which must be recognized in the usual way, except that the replacement text of entities used to escape markup delimiters (the entities `amp`, `lt`, `gt`, `apos`, `quot`) is always treated as data. (The string "AT&T;" expands to "AT&T;" and the remaining ampersand is not recognized as an entity-reference delimiter.) A character reference is **included** when the indicated character is processed in place of the reference itself.

4.4.3 INCLUDED IF VALIDATING

When an XML processor recognizes a reference to a parsed entity, in order to validate the document, the processor must include its replacement text. If the entity is external, and the processor is not attempting to validate the XML document, the processor may, but need not, include the entity's replacement text. If a non-validating parser does not include the replacement text, it must inform the application that it recognized, but did not read, the entity.

This rule is based on the recognition that the automatic inclusion provided by the SGML and XML entity mechanism, primarily designed to support modularity in authoring, is not necessarily appropriate for other applications, in particular document browsing. Browsers, for example, when encountering an external parsed entity reference, might choose to provide a visual indication of the entity's presence and retrieve it for display only on demand.

4.4.4 FORBIDDEN

The following are forbidden, and constitute fatal errors:

- the appearance of a reference to an unparsed entity.
- the appearance of any character or general-entity reference in the DTD except within an `EntityValue` or `AttValue`.
- a reference to an external entity in an attribute value.

4.4.5 INCLUDED IN LITERAL

When an entity reference appears in an attribute value, or a parameter entity reference appears in a literal entity value, its replacement text is processed in place of the reference itself as though it were part of the document at the location the reference was recognized, except that a single or double quote character in the replacement text is always treated as a normal data character and will not terminate the literal. For example, this is well-formed:

```
<!ENTITY % YN '"Yes"' >
<!ENTITY WhatHeSaid "He said &YN;" >
```

while this is not:

```
<!ENTITY EndAttr "27'" >
<element attribute='a-&EndAttr;'>
```

4.4.6 NOTIFY

When the name of an unparsed entity appears as a token in the value of an attribute of declared type ENTITY or ENTITIES, a validating processor must inform the application of the system and public (if any) identifiers for both the entity and its associated notation.

4.4.7 BYPASSED

When a general entity reference appears in the EntityValue in an entity declaration, it is bypassed and left as is.

4.4.8 INCLUDED AS PE

Just as with external parsed entities, parameter entities need only be included if validating. When a parameter-entity reference is recognized in the DTD and included, its replacement text is enlarged by the attachment of one leading and one following space (#x20) character; the intent is to constrain the replacement text of parameter entities to contain an integral number of grammatical tokens in the DTD.

4.5 Construction of Internal Entity Replacement Text

In discussing the treatment of internal entities, it is useful to distinguish two forms of the entity's value. The **literal entity value** is the quoted string actually present in the entity declaration, corresponding to the nonterminal EntityValue. The **replacement text** is the content of the entity, after replacement of character references and parameter-entity references.

The literal entity value as given in an internal entity declaration (`EntityValue`) may contain character, parameter-entity, and general-entity references. Such references must be contained entirely within the literal entity value. The actual replacement text that is included as described above must contain the *replacement text* of any parameter entities referred to, and must contain the character referred to, in place of any character references in the literal entity value; however, general-entity references must be left as-is, unexpanded. For example, given the following declarations:

```
<!ENTITY % pub     "&#xc9;ditions Gallimard" >
<!ENTITY   rights "All rights reserved" >
<!ENTITY   book   "La Peste: Albert Camus,
&#xA9; 1947 %pub;. &rights;" >
```

then the replacement text for the entity "`book`" is:

```
La Peste: Albert Camus,
© 1947 Éditions Gallimard. &rights;
```

The general-entity reference "`&rights;`" would be expanded should the reference "`&book;`" appear in the document's content or an attribute value.

These simple rules may have complex interactions; for a detailed discussion of a difficult example, see "D. Expansion of Entity and Character References".

4.6 Predefined Entities

Entity and character references can both be used to **escape** the left angle bracket, ampersand, and other delimiters. A set of general entities (`amp`, `lt`, `gt`, `apos`, `quot`) is specified for this purpose. Numeric character references may also be used; they are expanded immediately when recognized and must be treated as character data, so the numeric character references "`&#60;`" and "`&#38;`" may be used to escape < and & when they occur in character data.

All XML processors must recognize these entities whether they are declared or not. For interoperability, valid XML documents should declare these entities, like any others, before using them.

If the entities in question are declared, they must be declared as internal entities whose replacement text is the single character being escaped or a character reference to that character, as shown below.

```
<!ENTITY lt     "&#38;#60;">
<!ENTITY gt     "&#62;">
<!ENTITY amp    "&#38;#38;">
<!ENTITY apos   "&#39;">
<!ENTITY quot   "&#34;">
```

Note that the < and & characters in the declarations of "lt" and "amp" are doubly escaped to meet the requirement that entity replacement be well-formed.

4.7 Notation Declarations

Notations identify by name the format of unparsed entities, the format of elements which bear a notation attribute, or the application to which a processing instruction is addressed.

Notation declarations provide a name for the notation, for use in entity and attribute-list declarations and in attribute specifications, and an external identifier for the notation which may allow an XML processor or its client application to locate a helper application capable of processing data in the given notation.

NOTATION DECLARATIONS

```
[82] NotationDecl ::= '<!NOTATION'  S  Name S (ExternalID |
                       PublicID) S? '>'
[83]      PublicID ::= 'PUBLIC' S PubidLiteral
```

XML processors must provide applications with the name and external identifier(s) of any notation declared and referred to in an attribute value, attribute definition, or entity declaration. They may additionally resolve the external identifier into the system identifier, filename, or other information needed to allow the application to call a processor for data in the notation described. (It is not an error, however, for XML documents to declare and refer to notations for which notation-specific applications are not available on the system where the XML processor or application is running.)

4.8 Document Entity

The **document entity** serves as the root of the entity tree and a starting-point for an XML processor. This specification does not specify how the document entity is to be located by an XML processor; unlike other entities, the document entity has no name and might well appear on a processor input stream without any identification at all.

5. Conformance

5.1 Validating and Non-Validating Processors

Conforming XML processors fall into two classes: validating and non-validating.

Validating and non-validating processors alike must report violations of this specification's well-formedness constraints in the content of the document entity and any other parsed entities that they read.

Validating processors must report violations of the constraints expressed by the declarations in the DTD, and failures to fulfill the validity constraints given in this specification. To accomplish this, validating XML processors must read and process the entire DTD and all external parsed entities referenced in the document.

Non-validating processors are required to check only the document entity, including the entire internal DTD subset, for well-formedness. While they are not required to check the document for validity, they are required to **process** all the declarations they read in the internal DTD subset and in any parameter entity that they read, up to the first reference to a parameter entity that they do not read; that is to say, they must use the information in those declarations to normalize attribute values, include the replacement text of internal entities, and supply default attribute values. They must not process entity declarations or attribute-list declarations encountered after a reference to a parameter entity that is not read, since the entity may have contained overriding declarations.

5.2 Using XML Processors

The behavior of a validating XML processor is highly predictable; it must read every piece of a document and report all well-formedness and validity violations. Less is required of a non-validating processor; it need not read any part of the document other than the document entity. This has two effects that may be important to users of XML processors:

- Certain well-formedness errors, specifically those that require reading external entities, may not be detected by a non-validating processor. Examples include the constraints entitled Entity Declared, Parsed Entity, and No Recursion, as well as some of the cases described as forbidden in "4.4 XML Processor Treatment of Entities and References".
- The information passed from the processor to the application may vary, depending on whether the processor reads parameter and external entities. For example, a non-validating processor may not normalize attribute values, include the replacement text of internal entities, or supply default attribute values, where doing so depends on having read declarations in external or parameter entities.

For maximum reliability in interoperating between different XML processors, applications which use non-validating processors should not rely on any behaviors not required of such processors. Applications which require facilities such as the use of default attributes or internal entities which are declared in external entities should use validating XML processors.

6. Notation

The formal grammar of XML is given in this specification using a simple Extended Backus-Naur Form (EBNF) notation. Each rule in the grammar defines one symbol, in the form

```
symbol ::= expression
```

Symbols are written with an initial capital letter if they are defined by a regular expression, or with an initial lower case letter otherwise. Literal strings are quoted.

Within the expression on the right-hand side of a rule, the following expressions are used to match strings of one or more characters:

#xN

where N is a hexadecimal integer, the expression matches the character in ISO/IEC 10646 whose canonical (UCS-4) code value, when interpreted as an unsigned binary number, has the value indicated. The number of leading zeros in the #xN form is insignificant; the number of leading zeros in the corresponding code value is governed by the character encoding in use and is not significant for XML.

[a-zA-Z], [#xN-#xN]

matches any character with a value in the range(s) indicated (inclusive).

[^a-z], [^#xN-#xN]

matches any character with a value outside the range indicated.

[^abc], [^#xN#xN#xN]

matches any character with a value not among the characters given.

"string"

matches a literal string matching that given inside the double quotes.

'string'

matches a literal string matching that given inside the single quotes.

These symbols may be combined to match more complex patterns as follows, where A and B represent simple expressions:

(expression)

expression is treated as a unit and may be combined as described in this list.

A?

matches A or nothing; optional A.

A B

matches A followed by B.

A | B

matches A or B but not both.

A - B

matches any string that matches A but does not match B.

A+

matches one or more occurrences of A.

A*

matches zero or more occurrences of A.

Other notations used in the productions are:

`/* ... */`

comment.

`[ wfc: ... ]`

well-formedness constraint; this identifies by name a constraint on well-formed documents associated with a production.

`[ vc: ... ]`

validity constraint; this identifies by name a constraint on valid documents associated with a production.

Appendices

A. References

A.1 Normative References

IANA
(Internet Assigned Numbers Authority) *Official Names for Character Sets*, ed. Keld Simonsen et al. See *ftp://ftp.isi.edu/in-notes/iana/assignments/character-sets*.

IETF RFC 1766
IETF (Internet Engineering Task Force). *RFC 1766: Tags for the Identification of Languages*, ed. H. Alvestrand. 1995.

ISO 639
(International Organization for Standardization). *ISO 639:1988 (E). Code for the representation of names of languages*. [Geneva]: International Organization for Standardization, 1988.

ISO 3166
(International Organization for Standardization). *ISO 3166-1:1997 (E). Codes for the representation of names of countries and their subdivisions — Part 1: Country codes* [Geneva]: International Organization for Standardization, 1997.

ISO/IEC 10646
ISO (International Organization for Standardization). *ISO/IEC 10646-1993 (E). Information technology — Universal Multiple-Octet Coded Character Set (UCS) — Part 1: Architecture and Basic Multilingual Plane*. [Geneva]: International Organization for Standardization, 1993 (plus amendments AM 1 through AM 7).

Unicode
The Unicode Consortium. *The Unicode Standard, Version 2.0.* Reading, Mass.: Addison-Wesley Developers Press, 1996.

A.2 Other References

Aho/Ullman
Aho, Alfred V., Ravi Sethi, and Jeffrey D. Ullman. *Compilers: Principles, Techniques, and Tools.* Reading: Addison-Wesley, 1986, rpt. corr. 1988.

Berners-Lee et al.
  Berners-Lee, T., R. Fielding, and L. Masinter. *Uniform Resource Identifiers (URI): Generic Syntax and Semantics.* 1997. (Work in progress; see updates to RFC1738.)
Brüggemann-Klein
  Brüggemann-Klein, Anne. *Regular Expressions into Finite Automata.* Extended abstract in I. Simon, Hrsg., LATIN 1992, S. 97-98. Springer-Verlag, Berlin 1992. Full Version in Theoretical Computer Science 120: 197-213, 1993.
Brüggemann-Klein and Wood
  Brüggemann-Klein, Anne, and Derick Wood. *Deterministic Regular Languages.* Universität Freiburg, Institut für Informatik, Bericht 38, Oktober 1991.
Clark
  James Clark. Comparison of SGML and XML. See *http://www. w3.org/TR/NOTE-sgml-xml-971215.*
IETF RFC1738
  IETF (Internet Engineering Task Force). RFC 1738: *Uniform Resource Locators (URL)*, ed. T. Berners-Lee, L. Masinter, M. McCahill. 1994.
IETF RFC1808
  IETF (Internet Engineering Task Force). *RFC 1808: Relative Uniform Resource Locators*, ed. R. Fielding. 1995.
IETF RFC2141
  IETF (Internet Engineering Task Force). RFC 2141: *URN Syntax*, ed. R. Moats. 1997.
ISO 8879
  ISO (International Organization for Standardization). *ISO 8879:1986(E). Information processing—Text and Office Systems—Standard Generalized Markup Language (SGML).* First edition—1986-10-15. [Geneva]: International Organization for Standardization, 1986.
ISO/IEC 10744
  ISO (International Organization for Standardization). *ISO/ IEC 10744-1992 (E). Information technology—Hypermedia/ Time-based Structuring Language (HyTime).* [Geneva]: International Organization for Standardization, 1992. *Extended Facilities Annexe.* [Geneva]: International Organization for Standardization, 1996.

B. Character Classes

Following the characteristics defined in the Unicode standard, characters are classed as base characters (among others, these contain the alphabetic characters of the Latin alphabet, without diacritics), ideographic characters, and combining characters (among others, this class contains most diacritics); these classes combine to form the class of letters. Digits and extenders are also distinguished.

CHARACTERS

```
[84]    Letter ::= BaseChar | Ideographic
[85]      BaseChar ::= [#x0041-#x005A]        | [#x0061-#x007A]
                     | [#x00C0-#x00D6]        | [#x00D8-#x00F6]
                     | [#x00F8-#x00FF]        | [#x0100-#x0131]
                     | [#x0134-#x013E]        | [#x0141-#x0148]
                     | [#x014A-#x017E]        | [#x0180-#x01C3]
                     | [#x01CD-#x01F0]        | [#x01F4-#x01F5]
                     | [#x01FA-#x0217]        | [#x0250-#x02A8]
                     | [#x02BB-#x02C1]   | #x0386  | [#x0388-
                     #x038A]       | #x038C   | [#x038E-#x03A1]
                     | [#x03A3-#x03CE]        | [#x03D0-#x03D6]
                     | #x03DA   | #x03DC   | #x03DE  | #x03E0
                     | [#x03E2-#x03F3]        | [#x0401-#x040C]
                     | [#x040E-#x044F]        | [#x0451-#x045C]
                     | [#x045E-#x0481]        | [#x0490-#x04C4]
                     | [#x04C7-#x04C8]        | [#x04CB-#x04CC]
                     | [#x04D0-#x04EB]        | [#x04EE-#x04F5]
                     | [#x04F8-#x04F9]        | [#x0531-#x0556]
                     | #x0559   | [#x0561-#x0586]    | [#x05D0-
                     #x05EA]    | [#x05F0-#x05F2]     | [#x0621-
                     #x063A]    | [#x0641-#x064A]     | [#x0671-
                     #x06B7]    | [#x06BA-#x06BE]     | [#x06C0-
                     #x06CE]    | [#x06D0-#x06D3]     | #x06D5
                     | [#x06E5-#x06E6]        | [#x0905-#x0939]
                     | #x093D   | [#x0958-#x0961]    | [#x0985-
                     #x098C]    | [#x098F-#x0990]     | [#x0993-
                     #x09A8]    | [#x09AA-#x09B0]     | #x09B2
                     | [#x09B6-#x09B9]        | [#x09DC-#x09DD]
                     | [#x09DF-#x09E1]        | [#x09F0-#x09F1]
                     | [#x0A05-#x0A0A]        | [#x0A0F-#x0A10]
                     | [#x0A13-#x0A28]        | [#x0A2A-#x0A30]
                     | [#x0A32-#x0A33]        | [#x0A35-#x0A36]
                     | [#x0A38-#x0A39]        | [#x0A59-#x0A5C]
                     | #x0A5E   | [#x0A72-#x0A74]    | [#x0A85-
                     #x0A8B]    | #x0A8D    | [#x0A8F-#x0A91]
```

```
| [#x0A93-#x0AA8]        | [#x0AAA-#x0AB0]
| [#x0AB2-#x0AB3]        | [#x0AB5-#x0AB9]
| #x0ABD  | #x0AE0       | [#x0B05-#x0B0C]
| [#x0B0F-#x0B10]        | [#x0B13-#x0B28]
| [#x0B2A-#x0B30]        | [#x0B32-#x0B33]
| [#x0B36-#x0B39]  | #x0B3D  | [#x0B5C-
#x0B5D]  | [#x0B5F-#x0B61]        | [#x0B85-
#x0B8A]  | [#x0B8E-#x0B90]        | [#x0B92-
#x0B95]  | [#x0B99-#x0B9A]        | #x0B9C
| [#x0B9E-#x0B9F]        | [#x0BA3-#x0BA4]
| [#x0BA8-#x0BAA]        | [#x0BAE-#x0BB5]
| [#x0BB7-#x0BB9]        | [#x0C05-#x0C0C]
| [#x0C0E-#x0C10]        | [#x0C12-#x0C28]
| [#x0C2A-#x0C33]        | [#x0C35-#x0C39]
| [#x0C60-#x0C61]        | [#x0C85-#x0C8C]
| [#x0C8E-#x0C90]        | [#x0C92-#x0CA8]
| [#x0CAA-#x0CB3]        | [#x0CB5-#x0CB9]
| #x0CDE  | [#x0CE0-#x0CE1]  | [#x0D05-
#x0D0C]  | [#x0D0E-#x0D10]  | [#x0D12-
#x0D28]  | [#x0D2A-#x0D39]  | [#x0D60-
#x0D61]  | [#x0E01-#x0E2E]  | #x0E30
| [#x0E32-#x0E33]        | [#x0E40-#x0E45]
| [#x0E81-#x0E82]  | #x0E84  | [#x0E87-
#x0E88]  | #x0E8A  | #x0E8D  | [#x0E94-
#x0E97]  | [#x0E99-#x0E9F]        | [#x0EA1-
#x0EA3]  | #x0EA5  | #x0EA7  | [#x0EAA-
#x0EAB]  | [#x0EAD-#x0EAE]  | #x0EB0
| [#x0EB2-#x0EB3]  | #x0EBD  | [#x0EC0-
#x0EC4]  | [#x0F40-#x0F47]  | [#x0F49-
#x0F69]  | [#x10A0-#x10C5]  | [#x10D0-
#x10F6]  | #x1100  | [#x1102-#x1103]
| [#x1105-#x1107]  | #x1109  | [#x110B-
#x110C]  | [#x110E-#x1112]  | #x113C
| #x113E  | #x1140  | #x114C  | #x114E
| #x1150  | [#x1154-#x1155]  | #x1159
| [#x115F-#x1161]  | #x1163  | #x1165
| #x1167  | #x1169  | [#x116D-#x116E]
| [#x1172-#x1173]  | #x1175  | #x119E
| #x11A8  | #x11AB  | [#x11AE-#x11AF]
| [#x11B7-#x11B8]  | #x11BA  | [#x11BC-
#x11C2]  | #x11EB  | #x11F0  | #x11F9
| [#x1E00-#x1E9B]        | [#x1EA0-#x1EF9]
| [#x1F00-#x1F15]        | [#x1F18-#x1F1D]
| [#x1F20-#x1F45]        | [#x1F48-#x1F4D]
| [#x1F50-#x1F57]  | #x1F59  | #x1F5B
| #x1F5D  | [#x1F5F-#x1F7D]  | [#x1F80-
#x1FB4]  | [#x1FB6-#x1FBC]  | #x1FBE
| [#x1FC2-#x1FC4]        | [#x1FC6-#x1FCC]
| [#x1FD0-#x1FD3]        | [#x1FD6-#x1FDB]
```

(continued)

```
                                  |  [#x1FE0-#x1FEC]        |  [#x1FF2-#x1FF4]
                                  |  [#x1FF6-#x1FFC]  |  #x2126  |  [#x212A-
                            #x212B]    |  #x212E     |  [#x2180-#x2182]
                                  |  [#x3041-#x3094]        |  [#x30A1-#x30FA]
                                  |  [#x3105-#x312C]  |  [#xAC00-#xD7A3]
        [86]    Ideographic ::= [#x4E00-#x9FA5]       |  #x3007  |  [#x3021-
                            #x3029]
        [87] CombiningChar ::= [#x0300-#x0345]              |  [#x0360-#x0361]
                                  |  [#x0483-#x0486]        |  [#x0591-#x05A1]
                                  |  [#x05A3-#x05B9]        |  [#x05BB-#x05BD]
                                  |  #x05BF      |  [#x05C1-#x05C2]   |  #x05C4
                                  |  [#x064B-#x0652]  |  #x0670  |  [#x06D6-
                            #x06DC]  |  [#x06DD-#x06DF]        |  [#x06E0-
                            #x06E4]  |  [#x06E7-#x06E8]        |  [#x06EA-
                            #x06ED]    |  [#x0901-#x0903]        |  #x093C
                                  |  [#x093E-#x094C]  |  #x094D      |  [#x0951-
                            #x0954]  |  [#x0962-#x0963]        |  [#x0981-
                            #x0983]    |  #x09BC    |  #x09BE    |  #x09BF
                                  |  [#x09C0-#x09C4]        |  [#x09C7-#x09C8]
                                  |  [#x09CB-#x09CD]  |  #x09D7  |  [#x09E2-
                            #x09E3]    |  #x0A02    |  #x0A3C    |  #x0A3E
                                  |  #x0A3F    |  [#x0A40-#x0A42]    |  [#x0A47-
                            #x0A48]  |  [#x0A4B-#x0A4D]        |  [#x0A70-
                            #x0A71]    |  [#x0A81-#x0A83]        |  #x0ABC
                                  |  [#x0ABE-#x0AC5]        |  [#x0AC7-#x0AC9]
                                  |  [#x0ACB-#x0ACD]        |  [#x0B01-#x0B03]
                                  |  #x0B3C    |  [#x0B3E-#x0B43]    |  [#x0B47-
                            #x0B48]  |  [#x0B4B-#x0B4D]        |  [#x0B56-
                            #x0B57]  |  [#x0B82-#x0B83]        |  [#x0BBE-
                            #x0BC2]    |  [#x0BC6-#x0BC8]        |  [#x0BCA-
                            #x0BCD]    |  #x0BD7      |  [#x0C01-#x0C03]
                                  |  [#x0C3E-#x0C44]        |  [#x0C46-#x0C48]
                                  |  [#x0C4A-#x0C4D]        |  [#x0C55-#x0C56]
                                  |  [#x0C82-#x0C83]        |  [#x0CBE-#x0CC4]
                                  |  [#x0CC6-#x0CC8]        |  [#x0CCA-#x0CCD]
                                  |  [#x0CD5-#x0CD6]        |  [#x0D02-#x0D03]
                                  |  [#x0D3E-#x0D43]        |  [#x0D46-#x0D48]
                                  |  [#x0D4A-#x0D4D]      |  #x0D57    |  #x0E31
                                  |  [#x0E34-#x0E3A]        |  [#x0E47-#x0E4E]
                                  |  #x0EB1    |  [#x0EB4-#x0EB9]  |  [#x0EBB-
                            #x0EBC]  |  [#x0EC8-#x0ECD]        |  [#x0F18-
                            #x0F19]  |  #x0F35    |  #x0F37    |  #x0F39
                                  |  #x0F3E    |  #x0F3F    |  [#x0F71-#x0F84]
                                  |  [#x0F86-#x0F8B]        |  [#x0F90-#x0F95]
                                  |  #x0F97    |  [#x0F99-#x0FAD]    |  [#x0FB1-
                            #x0FB7]    |  #x0FB9    |  [#x20D0-#x20DC]
                                  |  #x20E1    |  [#x302A-#x302F]    |  #x3099
                                  |  #x309A
        [88]            Digit ::= [#x0030-#x0039]        |  [#x0660-#x0669]
                                  |  [#x06F0-#x06F9]        |  [#x0966-#x096F]
                                  |  [#x09E6-#x09EF]        |  [#x0A66-#x0A6F]
```

```
                       | [#x0AE6-#x0AEF]        | [#x0B66-#x0B6F]
                       | [#x0BE7-#x0BEF]        | [#x0C66-#x0C6F]
                       | [#x0CE6-#x0CEF]        | [#x0D66-#x0D6F]
                       | [#x0E50-#x0E59]        | [#x0ED0-#x0ED9]
                       | [#x0F20-#x0F29]
[89]      Extender ::= #x00B7   | #x02D0   | #x02D1   | #x0387
                       | #x0640  | #x0E46   | #x0EC6   |
#x3005
                       | [#x3031-#x3035]        | [#x309D-#x309E]
                       | [#x30FC-#x30FE]
```

The character classes defined here can be derived from the Unicode character database as follows:

- Name start characters must have one of the categories Ll, Lu, Lo, Lt, Nl.
- Name characters other than Name-start characters must have one of the categories Mc, Me, Mn, Lm, or Nd.
- Characters in the compatibility area (i.e. with character code greater than #xF900 and less than #xFFFE) are not allowed in XML names.
- Characters which have a font or compatibility decomposition (i.e. those with a "compatibility formatting tag" in field 5 of the database — marked by field 5 beginning with a "<") are not allowed.
- The following characters are treated as name-start characters rather than name characters, because the property file classifies them as Alphabetic: [#x02BB-#x02C1], #x0559, #x06E5, #x06E6.
- Characters #x20DD-#x20E0 are excluded (in accordance with Unicode, section 5.14).
- Character #x00B7 is classified as an extender, because the property list so identifies it.
- Character #x0387 is added as a name character, because #x00B7 is its canonical equivalent.
- Characters ':' and '_' are allowed as name-start characters.
- Characters '-' and '.' are allowed as name characters.

C. XML and SGML (Non-Normative)

XML is designed to be a subset of SGML, in that every valid XML document should also be a conformant SGML document. For a detailed comparison of the additional restrictions that XML places on documents beyond those of SGML, see [Clark].

D. Expansion of Entity and Character References (Non-Normative)

This appendix contains some examples illustrating the sequence of entity- and character-reference recognition and expansion, as specified in "4.4 XML Processor Treatment of Entities and References".

   If the DTD contains the declaration

```
<!ENTITY example "<p>An ampersand (&#38;#38;) may be escaped
numerically (&#38;#38;#38;) or with a general entity
(&amp;amp;).</p>" >
```

then the XML processor will recognize the character references when it parses the entity declaration, and resolve them before storing the following string as the value of the entity "example":

```
<p>An ampersand (&#38;) may be escaped
numerically (&#38;#38;) or with a general entity
(&amp;amp;).</p>
```

A reference in the document to "&example;" will cause the text to be reparsed, at which time the start- and end-tags of the "p" element will be recognized and the three references will be recognized and expanded, resulting in a "p" element with the following content (all data, no delimiters or markup):

```
An ampersand (&) may be escaped
numerically (&#38;) or with a general entity
(&amp;).
```

A more complex example will illustrate the rules and their effects fully. In the following example, the line numbers are solely for reference.

```
1  <?xml version='1.0'?>
2  <!DOCTYPE test [
3  <!ELEMENT test (#PCDATA) >
4  <!ENTITY % xx '&#37;zz;'>
5  <!ENTITY % zz '&#60;!ENTITY tricky "error-prone" >' >
6  %xx;
7  ]>
8  <test>This sample shows a &tricky; method.</test>
```

This produces the following:

- in line 4, the reference to character 37 is expanded immediately, and the parameter entity "xx" is stored in the symbol table with the value "%zz;". Since the replacement text is not rescanned, the reference to parameter entity "zz" is not recognized. (And it would be an error if it were, since "zz" is not yet declared.)

- in line 5, the character reference "<" is expanded immediately and the parameter entity "zz" is stored with the replacement text "<!ENTITY tricky "error-prone" >", which is a well-formed entity declaration.

- in line 6, the reference to "xx" is recognized, and the replacement text of "xx" (namely "%zz;") is parsed. The reference to "zz" is recognized in its turn, and its replacement text ("<!ENTITY tricky "error-prone" >") is parsed. The general entity "tricky" has now been declared, with the replacement text "error-prone".

- in line 8, the reference to the general entity "tricky" is recognized, and it is expanded, so the full content of the "test" element is the self-describing (and ungrammatical) string *This sample shows a error-prone method.*

E. Deterministic Content Models (Non-Normative)

For compatibility, it is required that content models in element type declarations be deterministic.

SGML requires deterministic content models (it calls them "unambiguous"); XML processors built using SGML systems may flag non-deterministic content models as errors.

For example, the content model ((b, c) | (b, d)) is non-deterministic, because given an initial b the parser cannot know which b in the model is being matched without looking ahead to see which element follows the b. In this case, the two references to b can be collapsed into a single reference, making the model read (b, (c | d)). An initial b now clearly matches only a single name in the content model. The parser doesn't need to look ahead to see what follows; either c or d would be accepted.

More formally: a finite state automaton may be constructed from the content model using the standard algorithms, e.g. algorithm 3.5 in section 3.9 of Aho, Sethi, and Ullman [Aho/Ullman]. In many such algorithms, a follow set is constructed for each position in the regular expression (i.e., each leaf node in the syntax tree for the regular expression); if any position has a follow set in which more than one following position is labeled with the same element type name, then the content model is in error and may be reported as an error.

Algorithms exist which allow many but not all non-deterministic content models to be reduced automatically to equivalent deterministic models; see Brüggemann-Klein 1991 [Brüggemann-Klein].

F. Autodetection of Character Encodings (Non-Normative)

The XML encoding declaration functions as an internal label on each entity, indicating which character encoding is in use. Before an XML processor can read the internal label, however, it apparently has to know what character encoding is in use—which is what the internal label is trying to indicate. In the general case, this is a hopeless situation. It is not entirely hopeless in XML, however, because XML limits the general case in two ways: each implementation is assumed to support only a finite set of character encodings, and the XML encoding declaration is restricted in position and content in order to make it feasible to autodetect the character encoding in use in each entity in normal cases. Also, in many cases other sources of information are available in addition to the XML data stream itself. Two cases may be distinguished, depending on whether the XML entity is presented to the processor without, or with, any accompanying (external) information. We consider the first case first.

Because each XML entity not in UTF-8 or UTF-16 format *must* begin with an XML encoding declaration, in which the first characters must be '<?xml', any conforming processor can detect, after two to four octets of input, which of the following cases apply. In reading this list, it may help to know that in UCS-4, '<' is "#x0000003C" and '?' is "#x0000003F", and the Byte Order Mark required of UTF-16 data streams is "#xFEFF".

- 00 00 00 3C: UCS-4, big-endian machine (1234 order)
- 3C 00 00 00: UCS-4, little-endian machine (4321 order)
- 00 00 3C 00: UCS-4, unusual octet order (2143)
- 00 3C 00 00: UCS-4, unusual octet order (3412)
- FE FF: UTF-16, big-endian
- FF FE: UTF-16, little-endian
- 00 3C 00 3F: UTF-16, big-endian, no Byte Order Mark (and thus, strictly speaking, in error)
- 3C 00 3F 00: UTF-16, little-endian, no Byte Order Mark (and thus, strictly speaking, in error)
- 3C 3F 78 6D: UTF-8, ISO 646, ASCII, some part of ISO 8859, Shift-JIS, EUC, or any other 7-bit, 8-bit, or mixed-width encoding which ensures that the characters of ASCII have their normal positions, width, and values; the actual encoding declaration must be read to detect which of these applies, but since all of these encodings use the same bit patterns for the ASCII characters, the encoding declaration itself may be read reliably
- 4C 6F A7 94: EBCDIC (in some flavor; the full encoding declaration must be read to tell which code page is in use)
- other: UTF-8 without an encoding declaration, or else the data stream is corrupt, fragmentary, or enclosed in a wrapper of some kind

This level of autodetection is enough to read the XML encoding declaration and parse the character-encoding identifier, which is still necessary to distinguish the individual members of each family of encodings (e.g. to tell UTF-8 from 8859, and the parts of 8859 from each other, or to distinguish the specific EBCDIC code page in use, and so on).

Because the contents of the encoding declaration are restricted to ASCII characters, a processor can reliably read the entire encoding declaration as soon as it has detected which family of encodings is in use. Since in practice, all widely used character encodings fall into one of the categories above, the XML encoding declaration allows reasonably reliable in-band labeling of character encodings, even when external sources of information at the operating-system or transport-protocol level are unreliable.

Once the processor has detected the character encoding in use, it can act appropriately, whether by invoking a separate input routine for each case, or by calling the proper conversion function on each character of input.

Like any self-labeling system, the XML encoding declaration will not work if any software changes the entity's character set or encoding without updating the encoding declaration. Implementors of character-encoding routines should be careful to ensure the accuracy of the internal and external information used to label the entity.

The second possible case occurs when the XML entity is accompanied by encoding information, as in some file systems and some network protocols. When multiple sources of information are available, their relative priority and the preferred method of handling conflict should be specified as part of the higher-level protocol used to deliver XML. Rules for the relative priority of the internal label and the MIME-type label in an external header, for example, should be part of the RFC document defining the text/xml and application/xml MIME types. In the interests of interoperability, however, the following rules are recommended.

- If an XML entity is in a file, the Byte-Order Mark and encoding-declaration PI are used (if present) to determine the character encoding. All other heuristics and sources of information are solely for error recovery.
- If an XML entity is delivered with a MIME type of text/xml, then the `charset` parameter on the MIME type determines the character encoding method; all other heuristics and sources of information are solely for error recovery.
- If an XML entity is delivered with a MIME type of application/xml, then the Byte-Order Mark and encoding-declaration PI are used (if present) to determine the character encoding. All other heuristics and sources of information are solely for error recovery.

These rules apply only in the absence of protocol-level documentation; in particular, when the MIME types text/xml and application/xml are defined, the recommendations of the relevant RFC will supersede these rules.

G. W3C XML Working Group (Non-Normative)

This specification was prepared and approved for publication by the W3C XML Working Group (WG). WG approval of this specification does not necessarily imply that all WG members voted for its approval. The current and former members of the XML WG are:

Jon Bosak, Sun (Chair); James Clark (Technical Lead); Tim Bray, Textuality and Netscape (XML Co-editor); Jean Paoli, Microsoft (XML Co-editor); C. M. Sperberg-McQueen, U. of Ill. (XML Co-editor); Dan Connolly, W3C (W3C Liaison); Paula Angerstein, Texcel; Steve DeRose, INSO; Dave Hollander, HP; Eliot Kimber, ISOGEN; Eve Maler, ArborText; Tom Magliery, NCSA; Murray Maloney, Muzmo and Grif; Makoto Murata, Fuji Xerox Information Systems; Joel Nava, Adobe; Conleth O'Connell, Vignette; Peter Sharpe, SoftQuad; John Tigue, DataChannel.

C XHTML Specification

*T*his appendix shows the XHTML Specification 1.0.

◆ XHTML™ 1.0: The Extensible HyperText Markup Language

◆ A Reformulation of HTML 4 in XML 1.0

W3C Recommendation 26 January 2000

This version:
> *http://www.w3.org/TR/2000/REC-xhtml1-20000126*
> (Postscript version, PDF version, ZIP archive, or Gzip'd TAR archive)

Latest version:
> *http://www.w3.org/TR/xhtml1*

Previous version:
> *http://www.w3.org/TR/1999/PR-xhtml1-19991210*

Authors:
> See acknowledgments.

◆ Abstract

This specification defines XHTML 1.0, a reformulation of HTML 4 as an XML 1.0 application, and three DTDs corresponding to the ones defined by HTML 4. The semantics of the elements and their attributes are defined in the W3C Recommendation for HTML 4. These semantics provide the foundation for future extensibility of XHTML. Compatibility with existing HTML user agents is possible by following a small set of guidelines.

◆ Status of this document

This section describes the status of this document at the time of its publication. Other documents may supersede this document. The latest status of this document series is maintained at the W3C.

This document has been reviewed by W3C Members and other interested parties and has been endorsed by the Director as a W3C Recommendation. It is a stable document and may be used as reference material or cited as a normative reference from another document. W3C's role in making the Recommendation is to draw attention to the specification and to promote its widespread deployment. This enhances the functionality and interoperability of the Web.

This document has been produced as part of the W3C HTML Activity. The goals of the HTML Working Group (*members only*) are discussed in the HTML Working Group charter (*members only*).

A list of current W3C Recommendations and other technical documents can be found at *http://www.w3.org/TR*.

Public discussion on HTML features takes place on the mailing list *www-html@w3.org* (archive).

Please report errors in this document to *www-html-editor@ w3.org*.

The list of known errors in this specification is available at *http://www.w3.org/2000/01/REC-xhtml1-20000126-errata*.

◆ Contents

1. What is XHTML?
   1.1 What is HTML 4?

1. What is XHTML?

XHTML is a family of current and future document types and modules that reproduce, subset, and extend HTML 4 [HTML]. XHTML family document types are XML based, and ultimately are designed to work in conjunction with XML-based user agents. The details of this family and its evolution are discussed in more detail in the section on Future Directions.

XHTML 1.0 (this specification) is the first document type in the XHTML family. It is a reformulation of the three HTML 4 document types as applications of XML 1.0 [XML]. It is intended to be used as a language for content that is both XML-conforming and, if some simple guidelines are followed, operates in HTML 4 conforming user agents. Developers who migrate their content to XHTML 1.0 will realize the following benefits:

- XHTML documents are XML conforming. As such, they are readily viewed, edited, and validated with standard XML tools.

- XHTML documents can be written to to operate as well or better than they did before in existing HTML 4-conforming user agents as well as in new, XHTML 1.0 conforming user agents.
- XHTML documents can utilize applications (e.g. scripts and applets) that rely upon either the HTML Document Object Model or the XML Document Object Model [DOM].
- As the XHTML family evolves, documents conforming to XHTML 1.0 will be more likely to interoperate within and among various XHTML environments.

The XHTML family is the next step in the evolution of the Internet. By migrating to XHTML today, content developers can enter the XML world with all of its attendant benefits, while still remaining confident in their content's backward and future compatibility.

1.1 What is HTML 4?

HTML 4 [HTML] is an SGML (Standard Generalized Markup Language) application conforming to International Standard ISO 8879, and is widely regarded as the standard publishing language of the World Wide Web.

SGML is a language for describing markup languages, particularly those used in electronic document exchange, document management, and document publishing. HTML is an example of a language defined in SGML.

SGML has been around since the middle 1980's and has remained quite stable. Much of this stability stems from the fact that the language is both feature-rich and flexible. This flexibility, however, comes at a price, and that price is a level of complexity that has inhibited its adoption in a diversity of environments, including the World Wide Web.

HTML, as originally conceived, was to be a language for the exchange of scientific and other technical documents, suitable for use by non-document specialists. HTML addressed the problem of SGML complexity by specifying a small set of structural and semantic tags suitable for authoring relatively simple documents. In addition to simplifying the document structure, HTML added support for hypertext. Multimedia capabilities were added later.

In a remarkably short space of time, HTML became wildly popular and rapidly outgrew its original purpose. Since HTML's inception, there has been rapid invention of new elements for use within

HTML (as a standard) and for adapting HTML to vertical, highly specialized, markets. This plethora of new elements has led to compatibility problems for documents across different platforms.

As the heterogeneity of both software and platforms rapidly proliferate, it is clear that the suitability of 'classic' HTML 4 for use on these platforms is somewhat limited.

1.2 What is XML?

XML™ is the shorthand for Extensible Markup Language, and is an acronym of Extensible Markup Language [XML].

XML was conceived as a means of regaining the power and flexibility of SGML without most of its complexity. Although a restricted form of SGML, XML nonetheless preserves most of SGML's power and richness, and yet still retains all of SGML's commonly used features.

While retaining these beneficial features, XML removes many of the more complex features of SGML that make the authoring and design of suitable software both difficult and costly.

1.3 Why the need for XHTML?

The benefits of migrating to XHTML 1.0 are described above. Some of the benefits of migrating to XHTML in general are:

- Document developers and user agent designers are constantly discovering new ways to express their ideas through new markup. In XML, it is relatively easy to introduce new elements or additional element attributes. The XHTML family is designed to accommodate these extensions through XHTML modules and techniques for developing new XHTML-conforming modules (described in the forthcoming XHTML Modularization specification). These modules will permit the combination of existing and new feature sets when developing content and when designing new user agents.
- Alternate ways of accessing the Internet are constantly being introduced. Some estimates indicate that by the year 2002, 75% of Internet document viewing will be carried out on these alternate platforms. The XHTML family is designed with general user agent interoperability in mind. Through a new user agent and document profiling mechanism, servers, proxies, and user agents will be able to perform best effort

content transformation. Ultimately, it will be possible to develop XHTML-conforming content that is usable by any XHTML-conforming user agent.

2. Definitions

2.1 Terminology

The following terms are used in this specification. These terms extend the definitions in [RFC2119] in ways based upon similar definitions in ISO/IEC 9945-1:1990 [POSIX.1]:

Implementation-defined

A value or behavior is implementation-defined when it is left to the implementation to define [and document] the corresponding requirements for correct document construction.

May

With respect to implementations, the word "may" is to be interpreted as an optional feature that is not required in this specification but can be provided. With respect to Document Conformance, the word "may" means that the optional feature must not be used. The term "optional" has the same definition as "may".

Must

In this specification, the word "must" is to be interpreted as a mandatory requirement on the implementation or on Strictly Conforming XHTML Documents, depending upon the context. The term "shall" has the same definition as "must".

Reserved

A value or behavior is unspecified, but it is not allowed to be used by Conforming Documents nor to be supported by a Conforming User Agents.

Should

With respect to implementations, the word "should" is to be interpreted as an implementation recommendation, but not a requirement. With respect to documents, the word "should" is to be interpreted as recommended programming practice for documents and a requirement for Strictly Conforming XHTML Documents.

Supported

Certain facilities in this specification are optional. If a facility is supported, it behaves as specified by this specification.

Unspecified

When a value or behavior is unspecified, the specification defines no portability requirements for a facility on an implementation even when faced with a document that uses the facility. A document that requires specific behavior in such an instance, rather than tolerating any behavior when using that facility, is not a Strictly Conforming XHTML Document.

2.2 General Terms

Attribute

An attribute is a parameter to an element declared in the DTD. An attribute's type and value range, including a possible default value, are defined in the DTD.

DTD

A DTD, or document type definition, is a collection of XML declarations that, as a collection, defines the legal structure, *elements*, and *attributes* that are available for use in a document that complies to the DTD.

Document

A document is a stream of data that, after being combined with any other streams it references, is structured such that it holds information contained within *elements* that are organized as defined in the associated *DTD*. See Document Conformance for more information.

Element

An element is a document structuring unit declared in the *DTD*. The element's content model is defined in the *DTD*, and additional semantics may be defined in the prose description of the element.

Facilities

Functionality includes *elements, attributes,* and the semantics associated with those *elements* and *attributes*. An implementation supporting that functionality is said to provide the necessary facilities.

Implementation

An implementation is a system that provides collection of *facilities* and services that supports this specification. See User Agent Conformance for more information.

Parsing

Parsing is the act whereby a *document* is scanned, and the information contained within the *document* is filtered into the context of the *elements* in which the information is structured.

Rendering

Rendering is the act whereby the information in a *document* is presented. This presentation is done in the form most appropriate to the environment (e.g. aurally, visually, in print).

User Agent

A user agent is an *implementation* that retrieves and processes XHTML documents. See User Agent Conformance for more information.

Validation

Validation is a process whereby *documents* are verified against the associated *DTD*, ensuring that the structure, use of *elements*, and use of *attributes* are consistent with the definitions in the *DTD*.

Well-formed

A *document* is well-formed when it is structured according to the rules defined in Section 2.1 of the XML 1.0 Recommendation [XML]. Basically, this definition states that elements, delimited by their start and end tags, are nested properly within one another.

3. Normative Definition of XHTML 1.0

3.1 Document Conformance

This version of XHTML provides a definition of strictly conforming XHTML documents, which are restricted to tags and attributes from the XHTML namespace. See Section 3.1.2 for information on using XHTML with other namespaces, for instance, to include metadata expressed in RDF within XHTML documents.

3.1.1 STRICTLY CONFORMING DOCUMENTS

A Strictly Conforming XHTML Document is a document that requires only the facilities described as mandatory in this specification. Such a document must meet all of the following criteria:

1. It must validate against one of the three DTDs found in Appendix A.
2. The root element of the document must be <html>.
3. The root element of the document must designate the XHTML namespace using the xmlns attribute [XML-NAMES]. The namespace for XHTML is defined to be http://www.w3.org/1999/xhtml.

4. There must be a DOCTYPE declaration in the document prior to the root element. The public identifier included in the DOCTYPE declaration must reference one of the three DTDs found in Appendix A using the respective Formal Public Identifier. The system identifier may be changed to reflect local system conventions.

```
 5.    <!DOCTYPE html
 6.        PUBLIC "-//W3C//DTD XHTML 1.0
       Strict//EN"
 7.            "DTD/xhtml1-strict.dtd">
 8.
 9.    <!DOCTYPE html
10.        PUBLIC "-//W3C//DTD XHTML 1.0
       Transitional//EN"
11.            "DTD/xhtml1-transitional.dtd">
12.
13.    <!DOCTYPE html
14.        PUBLIC "-//W3C//DTD XHTML 1.0
       Frameset//EN"
15.            "DTD/xhtml1-frameset.dtd">
```

Here is an example of a minimal XHTML document.

```
<?xml version="1.0" encoding="UTF-8"?>
<!DOCTYPE html
     PUBLIC "-//W3C//DTD XHTML 1.0
Strict//EN"
     "DTD/xhtml1-strict.dtd">
<html xmlns="http://www.w3.org/1999/xhtml"
xml:lang="en" lang="en">
  <head>
    <title>Virtual Library</title>
  </head>
  <body>
    <p>Moved to <a href="http://vlib.org/">vlib.org</a>.</p>
  </body>
</html>
```

Note that in this example, the XML declaration is included. An XML declaration like the one above is not required in all XML documents. XHTML document authors are strongly encouraged to use XML declarations in all their documents. Such a declaration is required when the character encoding of the document is other than the default UTF-8 or UTF-16.

3.1.2 USING XHTML WITH OTHER NAMESPACES

The XHTML namespace may be used with other XML namespaces as per [XMLNAMES], although such documents are not strictly conforming XHTML 1.0 documents as defined above. Future work by W3C will address ways to specify conformance for documents involving multiple namespaces.

The following example shows the way in which XHTML 1.0 could be used in conjunction with the MathML Recommendation:

```
<html xmlns="http://www.w3.org/1999/xhtml"
xml:lang="en" lang="en">
  <head>
    <title>A Math Example</title>
  </head>
  <body>
    <p>The following is MathML
markup:</p>
    <math xmlns="http://www.w3.org/1998/Math/MathML">
      <apply> <log/>
        <logbase>
          <cn> 3 </cn>
        </logbase>
        <ci> x </ci>
      </apply>
    </math>
  </body>
</html>
```

The following example shows the way in which XHTML 1.0 markup could be incorporated into another XML namespace:

```
<?xml version="1.0" encoding="UTF-8"?>
<!- initially, the default namespace is "books" ->
<book xmlns='urn:loc.gov:books'
    xmlns:isbn='urn:ISBN:0-395-36341-6'
xml:lang="en" lang="en">
  <title>Cheaper by the Dozen</title>
  <isbn:number>1568491379</isbn:number>
  <notes>
    <!- make HTML the default namespace
for a hypertext commentary ->
    <p xmlns='http://www.w3.org/1999/xhtml'>
        This is also available <a
href="http://www.w3.org/">online</a>.
    </p>
  </notes>
</book>
```

3.2 User Agent Conformance

A conforming user agent must meet all of the following criteria:

1. In order to be consistent with the XML 1.0 Recommendation [XML], the user agent must parse and evaluate an XHTML document for well-formedness. If the user agent claims to be a validating user agent, it must also validate documents against their referenced DTDs according to [XML].

2. When the user agent claims to support facilities defined within this specification or required by this specification through normative reference, it must do so in ways consistent with the facilities' definition.

3. When a user agent processes an XHTML document as generic XML, it shall only recognize attributes of type ID (e.g., the id attribute on most XHTML elements) as fragment identifiers.

4. If a user agent encounters an element it does not recognize, it must render the element's content.

5. If a user agent encounters an attribute it does not recognize, it must ignore the entire attribute specification (i.e., the attribute and its value).

6. If a user agent encounters an attribute value it doesn't recognize, it must use the default attribute value.

7. If it encounters an entity reference (other than one of the predefined entities) for which the User Agent has processed no declaration (which could happen if the declaration is in the external subset which the User Agent hasn't read), the entity reference should be rendered as the characters (starting with the ampersand and ending with the semi-colon) that make up the entity reference.

8. When rendering content, User Agents that encounter characters or character entity references that are recognized but not renderable should display the document in such a way that it is obvious to the user that normal rendering has not taken place.

9. The following characters are defined in [XML] as whitespace characters:
   - Space ( )
   - Tab (	)
   - Carriage return ()
   - Line feed (
)

The XML processor normalizes different systems' line end codes into one single line-feed character that is passed up to the application. The XHTML user agent in addition must treat the following characters as whitespace:

- Form feed ()
- Zero-width space ()

In elements where the 'xml:space' attribute is set to 'preserve', the user agent must leave all whitespace characters intact (with the exception of leading and trailing whitespace characters, which should be removed). Otherwise, whitespace is handled according to the following rules:

- All whitespace surrounding block elements should be removed.
- Comments are removed entirely and do not affect whitespace handling. One whitespace character on either side of a comment is treated as two whitespace characters.
- Leading and trailing whitespace inside a block element must be removed.
- Line feed characters within a block element must be converted into a space (except when the 'xml:space' attribute is set to 'preserve').
- A sequence of whitespace characters must be reduced to a single space character (except when the 'xml:space' attribute is set to 'preserve').
- With regard to rendition, the User Agent should render the content in a manner appropriate to the language in which the content is written. In languages whose primary script is Latinate, the ASCII space character is typically used to encode both grammatical word boundaries and typographic whitespace; in languages whose script is related to Nagari (e.g., Sanskrit, Thai, etc.), grammatical boundaries may be encoded using the ZW 'space' character, but will not typically be represented by typographic whitespace in rendered output; languages using Arabiform scripts may encode typographic whitespace using a space character, but may also use the ZW space character to delimit 'internal' grammatical boundaries (what look like words in Arabic to an English eye frequently encode several words, e.g. 'kitAbuhum' = 'kitAbu-hum' = 'book them' = their book); and languages in the Chinese script tradition typically neither encode such delimiters nor use typographic whitespace in this way.

Whitespace in attribute values is processed according to [XML].

4. Differences with HTML 4

Due to the fact that XHTML is an XML application, certain practices that were perfectly legal in SGML-based HTML 4 [HTML] must be changed.

4.1 Documents must be well-formed

Well-formedness is a new concept introduced by [XML]. Essentially this means that all elements must either have closing tags or be written in a special form (as described below), and that all the elements must nest.

Although overlapping is illegal in SGML, it was widely tolerated in existing browsers.

CORRECT: nested elements.

```
<p>here is an emphasized
<em>paragraph</em>.</p>
```

INCORRECT: overlapping elements

```
<p>here is an emphasized
<em>paragraph.</p></em>
```

4.2 Element and attribute names must be in lower case

XHTML documents must use lower case for all HTML element and attribute names. This difference is necessary because XML is case-sensitive e.g. <li> and <LI> are different tags.

4.3 For non-empty elements, end tags are required

In SGML-based HTML 4 certain elements were permitted to omit the end tag; with the elements that followed implying closure. This omission is not permitted in XML-based XHTML. All elements other than those declared in the DTD as EMPTY must have an end tag.

CORRECT: terminated elements

<p>here is a paragraph.</p><p>here is another paragraph.</p>

INCORRECT: unterminated elements

<p>here is a paragraph.<p>here is another paragraph.

4.4 Attribute values must always be quoted

All attribute values must be quoted, even those which appear to be numeric.

CORRECT: quoted attribute values

<table rows="3">

INCORRECT: unquoted attribute values

<table rows=3>

4.5 Attribute Minimization

XML does not support attribute minimization. Attribute-value pairs must be written in full. Attribute names such as compact and checked cannot occur in elements without their value being specified.

CORRECT: unminimized attributes

<dl compact="compact">

INCORRECT: minimized attributes

<dl compact>

4.6 Empty Elements

Empty elements must either have an end tag or the start tag must end with />. For instance, <br/> or <hr></hr>. See HTML Compatibility Guidelines for information on ways to ensure this is backward compatible with HTML 4 user agents.

CORRECT: terminated empty tags

<hr/>

INCORRECT: unterminated empty tags

<hr>

4.7 Whitespace handling in attribute values

In attribute values, user agents will strip leading and trailing whitespace from attribute values and map sequences of one or more whitespace characters (including line breaks) to a single inter-word space (an ASCII space character for western scripts). See Section 3.3.3 of [XML].

4.8 Script and style elements

In XHTML, the script and style elements are declared as having #PCDATA content. As a result, < and & will be treated as the start of markup, and entities such as < and & will be recognized as entity references by the XML processor to < and & respectively. Wrapping the content of the script or style element within a CDATA marked section avoids the expansion of these entities.

```
<script>
 <![CDATA[
 ... unescaped script content ...
 ]]>
 </script>
```

CDATA sections are recognized by the XML processor and appear as nodes in the Document Object Model, see Section 1.3 of the DOM Level 1 Recommendation [DOM].
An alternative is to use external script and style documents.

4.9 SGML exclusions

SGML gives the writer of a DTD the ability to exclude specific elements from being contained within an element. Such prohibitions (called "exclusions") are not possible in XML.

For example, the HTML 4 Strict DTD forbids the nesting of an 'a' element within another 'a' element to any descendant depth. It is not possible to spell out such prohibitions in XML. Even though these prohibitions cannot be defined in the DTD, certain elements should not be nested. A summary of such elements and the elements that should not be nested in them is found in the normative Appendix B.

4.10 The elements with 'id' and 'name' attributes

HTML 4 defined the name attribute for the elements a, applet, form, frame, iframe, img, and map. HTML 4 also introduced the id attribute. Both of these attributes are designed to be used as fragment identifiers.

In XML, fragment identifiers are of type ID, and there can only be a single attribute of type ID per element. Therefore, in XHTML 1.0 the id attribute is defined to be of type ID. In order to ensure that XHTML 1.0 documents are well-structured XML documents, XHTML 1.0 documents MUST use the id attribute when defining fragment identifiers, even on elements that historically have also had a name attribute. See the HTML Compatibility Guidelines for information on ensuring such anchors are backwards compatible when serving XHTML documents as media type text/html.

Note that in XHTML 1.0, the name attribute of these elements is formally deprecated, and will be removed in a subsequent version of XHTML.

5. Compatibility Issues

Although there is no requirement for XHTML 1.0 documents to be compatible with existing user agents, in practice this is easy to accomplish. Guidelines for creating compatible documents can be found in Appendix C.

5.1 Internet Media Type

As of the publication of this recommendation, the general recommended MIME labeling for XML-based applications has yet to be resolved.

However, XHTML Documents which follow the guidelines set forth in Appendix C, "HTML Compatibility Guidelines" may be labeled with the Internet Media Type "text/html", as they are com-

patible with most HTML browsers. This document makes no recommendation about MIME labeling of other XHTML documents.

6. Future Directions

XHTML 1.0 provides the basis for a family of document types
that will extend and subset XHTML, in order to support a wide
range of new devices and applications, by defining modules and
specifying a mechanism for combining these modules. This
mechanism will enable the extension and subsetting of XHTML
1.0 in a uniform way through the definition of new modules.

6.1 Modularizing HTML

As the use of XHTML moves from the traditional desktop user
agents to other platforms, it is clear that not all of the XHTML elements will be required on all platforms. For example a hand
held device or a cellphone may only support a subset of XHTML
elements.

The process of modularization breaks XHTML up into a series
of smaller element sets. These elements can then be recombined
to meet the needs of different communities.

These modules will be defined in a later W3C document.

6.2 Subsets and Extensibility

Modularization brings with it several advantages:

- It provides a formal mechanism for subsetting XHTML.
- It provides a formal mechanism for extending XHTML.
- It simplifies the transformation between document types.
- It promotes the reuse of modules in new document types.

6.3 Document Profiles

A document profile specifies the syntax and semantics of a set of
documents. Conformance to a document profile provides a basis
for interoperability guarantees. The document profile specifies
the facilities required to process documents of that type, e.g.,
which image formats can be used, levels of scripting, style sheet
support, and so on.

For product designers this enables various groups to define
their own standard profile.

For authors this will obviate the need to write several different versions of documents for different clients.

For special groups such as chemists, medical doctors, or mathematicians this allows a special profile to be built using standard HTML elements plus a group of elements geared to the specialist's needs.

Appendix A. DTDs

This appendix is normative.

These DTDs and entity sets form a normative part of this specification. The complete set of DTD files together with an XML declaration and SGML Open Catalog is included in the zip file for this specification.

A.1 Document Type Definitions

These DTDs approximate the HTML 4 DTDs. It is likely that when the DTDs are modularized, a method of DTD construction will be employed that corresponds more closely to HTML 4.

- XHTML-1.0-Strict
- XHTML-1.0-Transitional
- XHTML-1.0-Frameset

A.2 Entity Sets

The XHTML entity sets are the same as for HTML 4, but have been modified to be valid XML 1.0 entity declarations. Note the entity for the Euro currency sign (`&euro;` or `&#8364;` or `&#x20AC;`) is defined as part of the special characters.

- Latin-1 characters
- Special characters
- Symbols

Appendix B. Element Prohibitions

This appendix is normative.

The following elements have prohibitions on which elements they can contain (see Section 4.9). This prohibition applies to all depths of nesting, i.e. it contains all the descendant elements.

`a`
cannot contain other `a` elements.

`pre`
cannot contain the `img`, `object`, `big`, `small`, `sub`, or `sup` elements.

`button`
cannot contain the `input`, `select`, `textarea`, `label`, `button`, `form`, `fieldset`, `iframe` or `isindex` elements.

`label`
cannot contain other `label` elements.

`form`
cannot contain other `form` elements.

Appendix C. HTML Compatibility Guidelines

This appendix is informative.

This appendix summarizes design guidelines for authors who wish their XHTML documents to render on existing HTML user agents.

C.1 Processing Instructions

Be aware that processing instructions are rendered on some user agents. However, also note that when the XML declaration is not included in a document, the document can only use the default character encodings UTF-8 or UTF-16.

C.2 Empty Elements

Include a space before the trailing / and > of empty elements, e.g., `<br />`, `<hr />` and `<img src="karen.jpg" alt="Karen" />`. Also, use the minimized tag syntax for empty elements, e.g., `<br />`, as the alternative syntax `<br></br>` allowed by XML gives uncertain results in many existing user agents.

C.3 Element Minimization and Empty Element Content

Given an empty instance of an element whose content model is not EMPTY (for example, an empty title or paragraph) do not use the minimized form (e.g. use `<p> </p>` and not `<p />`).

C.4 Embedded Style Sheets and Scripts

Use external style sheets if your style sheet uses < or & or]]> or --. Use external scripts if your script uses < or & or]]> or --. Note that XML parsers are permitted to silently remove the contents of comments. Therefore, the historical practice of "hiding" scripts and style sheets within comments to make the documents backward compatible is likely to not work as expected in XML-based implementations.

C.5 Line Breaks within Attribute Values

Avoid line breaks and multiple whitespace characters within attribute values. These are handled inconsistently by user agents.

C.6 Isindex

Don't include more than one `isindex` element in the document `head`. The `isindex` element is deprecated in favor of the `input` element.

C.7 The `lang` and `xml:lang` Attributes

Use both the `lang` and `xml:lang` attributes when specifying the language of an element. The value of the `xml:lang` attribute takes precedence.

C.8 Fragment Identifiers

In XML, URIs [RFC2396] that end with fragment identifiers of the form "#foo" do not refer to elements with an attribute name="foo"; rather, they refer to elements with an attribute defined to be of type ID, e.g., the `id` attribute in HTML 4. Many existing HTML clients don't support the use of ID-type attributes in this way, so identical values may be supplied for both of these attributes to ensure maximum forward and backward compatibility (e.g., `<a id="foo" name="foo">...</a>`).

Further, since the set of legal values for attributes of type ID is much smaller than for those of type CDATA, the type of the name attribute has been changed to NMTOKEN. This attribute is constrained such that it can only have the same values as type ID, or as the Name production in XML 1.0 Section 2.5, production 5. Unfortunately, this constraint cannot be expressed in the XHTML 1.0 DTDs. Because of this change, care must be taken when converting existing HTML documents. The values of these attributes must be unique within the document, valid, and any references to these fragment identifiers (both internal and external) must be updated should the values be changed during conversion.

Finally, note that XHTML 1.0 has deprecated the name attribute of the a, applet, form, frame, iframe, img, and map elements, and it will be removed from XHTML in subsequent versions.

C.9 Character Encoding

To specify a character encoding in the document, use both the encoding attribute specification on the xml declaration (e.g. `<?xml version="1.0" encoding="EUC-JP"?>`) and a meta http-equiv statement (e.g. `<meta http-equiv="Content-type" content='text/html; charset="EUC-JP"' />`). The value of the encoding attribute of the xml processing instruction takes precedence.

C.10 Boolean Attributes

Some HTML user agents are unable to interpret boolean attributes when these appear in their full (non-minimized) form, as required by XML 1.0. Note this problem doesn't affect user agents compliant with HTML 4. The following attributes are involved: compact, nowrap, ismap, declare, noshade, checked, disabled, readonly, multiple, selected, noresize, defer.

C.11 Document Object Model and XHTML

The Document Object Model level 1 Recommendation [DOM] defines document object model interfaces for XML and HTML 4. The HTML 4 document object model specifies that HTML element and attribute names are returned in upper-case. The XML document object model specifies that element and attribute names are returned in the case they are specified. In XHTML 1.0, elements and attributes are specified in lower-case. This apparent difference can be addressed in two ways:

1. Applications that access XHTML documents served as Internet media type text/html via the DOM can use the

HTML DOM, and can rely upon element and attribute names being returned in upper-case from those interfaces.

2. Applications that access XHTML documents served as Internet media types `text/xml` or `application/xml` can also use the XML DOM. Elements and attributes will be returned in lower-case. Also, some XHTML elements may or may not appear in the object tree because they are optional in the content model (e.g., the `tbody` element within `table`). This occurs because in HTML 4 some elements were permitted to be minimized such that their start and end tags are both omitted (an SGML feature). This is not possible in XML. Rather than require document authors to insert extraneous elements, XHTML has made the elements optional. Applications need to adapt to this accordingly.

C.12 Using Ampersands in Attribute Values

When an attribute value contains an ampersand, it must be expressed as a character entity reference (e.g. "`&amp;`"). For example, when the `href` attribute of the a element refers to a CGI script that takes parameters, it must be expressed as `http://my.site.dom/cgi-bin/myscript.pl?class=guest&amp;name=user` rather than as `http://my.site.dom/cgi-bin/myscript.pl?class=guest&name=user`.

C.13 Cascading Style Sheets (CSS) and XHTML

The Cascading Style Sheets level 2 Recommendation [CSS2] defines style properties which are applied to the parse tree of the HTML or XML document. Differences in parsing will produce different visual or aural results, depending on the selectors used. The following hints will reduce this effect for documents which are served without modification as both media types:

1. CSS style sheets for XHTML should use lowercase element and attribute names.
2. In tables, the tbody element will be inferred by the parser of an HTML user agent, but not by the parser of an XML user agent. Therefore you should always explicitly add a tbody element if it is referred to in a CSS selector.
3. Within the XHTML namespace, user agents are expected to recognize the "id" attribute as an attribute of type ID.

Therefore, style sheets should be able to continue using the shorthand "#" selector syntax even if the user agent does not read the DTD.

4. Within the XHTML name space, user agents are expected to recognize the "class" attribute. Therefore, style sheets should be able to continue using the shorthand "." selector syntax.

5. CSS defines different conformance rules for HTML and XML documents; be aware that the HTML rules apply to XHTML documents delivered as HTML and the XML rules apply to XHTML documents delivered as XML.

Appendix D. Acknowledgments

This appendix is informative.

This specification was written with the participation of the members of the W3C HTML working group:

Steven Pemberton, CWI (HTML Working Group Chair)

Murray Altheim, Sun Microsystems

Daniel Austin, AskJeeves (CNET: The Computer Network through July 1999)

Frank Boumphrey, HTML Writers Guild

John Burger, Mitre

Andrew W. Donoho, IBM

Sam Dooley, IBM

Klaus Hofrichter, GMD

Philipp Hoschka, W3C

Masayasu Ishikawa, W3C

Warner ten Kate, Philips Electronics

Peter King, Phone.com

Paula Klante, JetForm

Shin'ichi Matsui, Panasonic (W3C visiting engineer through September 1999)

Shane McCarron, Applied Testing and Technology (The Open Group through August 1999)

Ann Navarro, HTML Writers Guild

Zach Nies, Quark
Dave Raggett, W3C/HP (W3C lead for HTML)
Patrick Schmitz, Microsoft
Sebastian Schnitzenbaumer, Stack Overflow
Peter Stark, Phone.com
Chris Wilson, Microsoft
Ted Wugofski, Gateway 2000
Dan Zigmond, WebTV Networks

Appendix E. References

This appendix is informative.

[CSS2]
"Cascading Style Sheets, level 2 (CSS2) Specification", B. Bos, H. W. Lie, C. Lilley, I. Jacobs, 12 May 1998.
Latest version available at: *http://www.w3.org/TR/REC-CSS2*

[DOM]
"Document Object Model (DOM) Level 1 Specification", Lauren Wood *et al.*, 1 October 1998.
Latest version available at: *http://www.w3.org/TR/REC-DOM-Level-1*

[HTML]
"HTML 4.01 Specification", D. Raggett, A. Le Hors, I. Jacobs, 24 December 1999.
Latest version available at: *http://www.w3.org/TR/html401*

[POSIX.1]
"ISO/IEC 9945-1:1990 Information Technology - Portable Operating System Interface (POSIX) - Part 1: System Application Program Interface (API) [C Language]", Institute of Electrical and Electronics Engineers, Inc, 1990.

[RFC2046]
"RFC2046: Multipurpose Internet Mail Extensions (MIME) Part Two: Media Types", N. Freed and N. Borenstein, November 1996.
Available at *http://www.ietf.org/rfc/rfc2046.txt*. Note that this RFC obsoletes RFC1521, RFC1522, and RFC1590.

[RFC2119]
"RFC2119: Key words for use in RFCs to Indicate Requirement Levels", S. Bradner, March 1997.
Available at: *http://www.ietf.org/rfc/rfc2119.txt*

[RFC2376]

"RFC2376: XML Media Types", E. Whitehead, M. Murata, July 1998.
Available at: *http://www.ietf.org/rfc/rfc2376.txt*

[RFC2396]

"RFC2396: Uniform Resource Identifiers (URI): Generic Syntax", T. Berners-Lee, R. Fielding, L. Masinter, August 1998.
This document updates RFC1738 and RFC1808.
Available at: *http://www.ietf.org/rfc/rfc2396.txt*

[XML]

"Extensible Markup Language (XML) 1.0 Specification", T. Bray, J. Paoli, C. M. Sperberg-McQueen, 10 February 1998.
Latest version available at: *http://www.w3.org/TR/REC-xml*

[XMLNAMES]

"Namespaces in XML", T. Bray, D. Hollander, A. Layman, 14 January 1999.
XML namespaces provide a simple method for qualifying names used in XML documents by associating them with namespaces identified by URI.
Latest version available at: *http://www.w3.org/TR/REC-xml-names*

D Document Notice: W3C

*T*his appendix contains a document notice required for the reprinting of W3C documents. The full text of the notice is contained herein.

◆ Document Notice

Public documents on the W3C site are provided by the copyright holders under the following license. The software or Document Type Definitions (DTDs) associated with W3C specifications are governed by the Software Notice. By using and/or copying this document, or the W3C document from which this statement is linked, you (the licensee) agree that you have read, understood, and will comply with the following terms and conditions:

Permission to use, copy, and distribute the contents of this document, or the W3C document from which this statement is linked, in any medium for any purpose and without fee or royalty is hereby granted, provided that you include the following on ALL copies of the document, or portions thereof, that you use:

1. A link or URL to the original W3C document.
2. The pre-existing copyright notice of the original author, or if it doesn't exist, a notice of the form: "Copyright © [$date-of-document] World Wide Web Consortium,

(Massachusetts Institute of Technology, Institut National de Recherche en Informatique et en Automatique, Keio University). All Rights Reserved. *http://www.w3.org/ Consortium/Legal/"* (Hypertext is preferred, but a textual representation is permitted.)
3. *If it exists*, the STATUS of the W3C document.

When space permits, inclusion of the full text of this **NOTICE** should be provided. We request that authorship attribution be provided in any software, documents, or other items or products that you create pursuant to the implementation of the contents of this document, or any portion thereof.

No right to create modifications or derivatives of W3C documents is granted pursuant to this license. However, if additional requirements (documented in the Copyright FAQ) are satisfied, the right to create modifications or derivatives is sometimes granted by the W3C to individuals complying with those requirements.

THIS DOCUMENT IS PROVIDED "AS IS," AND COPYRIGHT HOLDERS MAKE NO REPRESENTATIONS OR WARRANTIES, EXPRESS OR IMPLIED, INCLUDING, BUT NOT LIMITED TO, WARRANTIES OF MERCHANTABILITY, FITNESS FOR A PARTICULAR PURPOSE, NONINFRINGEMENT, OR TITLE; THAT THE CONTENTS OF THE DOCUMENT ARE SUITABLE FOR ANY PURPOSE; NOR THAT THE IMPLEMENTATION OF SUCH CONTENTS WILL NOT INFRINGE ANY THIRD PARTY PATENTS, COPYRIGHTS, TRADEMARKS OR OTHER RIGHTS.

COPYRIGHT HOLDERS WILL NOT BE LIABLE FOR ANY DIRECT, INDIRECT, SPECIAL OR CONSEQUENTIAL DAMAGES ARISING OUT OF ANY USE OF THE DOCUMENT OR THE PERFORMANCE OR IMPLEMENTATION OF THE CONTENTS THEREOF.

The name and trademarks of copyright holders may NOT be used in advertising or publicity pertaining to this document or its contents without specific, written prior permission. Title to copyright in this document will at all times remain with copyright holders.

This formulation of W3C's notice and license became active on April 05 1999 so as to account for the treatment of DTDs, schemas and bindings. See the older formulation for the policy prior to this date. Please see our Copyright FAQ for common questions about using materials from our site, including specific terms and conditions for packages like libwww, Amaya, and Jigsaw. Other questions about this notice can be directed to *sitepolicy@w3.org*.

webmaster
(last updated by reagle on 1999/04/99.)

Glossary

A

adaptive dithering
A form of dithering in which the program looks to the image to determine the best set of colors when creating an 8-bit or smaller palette. See dithering.

aliasing
In bitmapped graphics, the jagged boundary along the edges of different-colored shapes within an image. See antialiasing.

antialiasing
A technique for reducing the jagged appearance of aliased bitmapped images, usually by inserting pixels that blend at the boundaries between adjacent colors.

artifacts
Image imperfections caused by compression.

authoring tools
Creation tools for interactive media.

AVI
AudioVideo Interleaved. Microsoft's file format for desktop video movies.

B

8-bit graphics
A color or grayscale graphic or movie that has 256 colors or less.

8-bit sounds
Eight-bit sounds have a dynamic range of 48 dB. Dynamic range is the measure of steps between the volume or amplitude of a sound.

16-bit graphics
A color image or movie that has 65.5 thousand colors.

16-bit sound

Standard CD-quality sound resolution, which has a dynamic range of 96 dB.

24-bit graphics

A color image or movie that has 16.7 million colors.

32-bit graphics

A color image or movie that has 16.7 million colors, plus an 8-bit masking channel.

bit depth

The number of bits used to represent the color of each pixel in a given movie or still image. Bit depth of 2 = black and white pixels. Bit depth of 4 = 16 colors or grays. Bit depth of 8 = 256 colors or grays. Bit depth of 16 = 65,536 colors. Bit depth of 24 = approximately 16 million colors.

bitmapped graphic (raster graphics)

A type of graphic image that is stored as a pattern of dots. With a paint program, the user can control how each dot of light (called a pixel) appears. The color of each pixel on-screen is stored as a series of bits, or 1s and 0s, which is why this type of graphic is called bitmapped (see object-oriented graphic).

browser

An application that enables you to access World Wide Web pages. Most browsers provide the capability to view Web pages, copy and print material from Web pages, download files over the Web, and navigate throughout the Web.

C

cache

A storage area that keeps frequently accessed data or program instructions readily available so that you do not have to retrieve them repeatedly.

CGI

Common Gateway Interface. A Web standard for the methods used by servers and external programs and scripts to communicate.

CSS

Cascading Style Sheets. A way of defining the appearance of particular HTML and/or XML elements.

client

A computer that requests information from a network's server (see server).

CLUT

Color Lookup Table. An 8-bit or lower image file uses a CLUT to define its palette.

codec

Compressor/decompressor. A piece of software that encodes and decodes movie data.

color mapping

A color map refers to the color palette of an image. Color mapping means assigning colors to an image.

compression

Reduction in the amount of data required to re-create an original file, graphic, or movie. Compression is used to reduce the transmission time of media and application files across the Web.

D

data streaming

The capability to delivery time-based data as it's requested, much like a VCR, rather than having to download all the information before it can be played.

dithering

The positioning of different colored pixels within an image that uses a 256-color palette to simulate a color that does not exist in the palette. A dithered image often looks noisy, or composed of scattered pixels (see adaptive dithering).

document type definition

The collection of markup declarations that describes an XML document's permissible elements and structure.

dynamic

Information that changes over a period of time. Typically refers to time-based media, such as animation or interactive documents.

DSSSL

The Document Style Semantics and Specification Language; ISO standard 10179:1996. An extremely powerful, extensible, and precise means of specifying exactly what you want to see on a printed page—generally used for formatting SGML documents.

E

entity

An unspecified type of storage unit for data (XML-related).

extension

Abbreviated code at the end of a file that tells the browser what kind of file it's looking at. Example: A JPEG file would have the extension .jpg.

external graphic

A graphic that must be downloaded from the Web instead of being viewed directly from a Web page. See inline graphic and links.

F

fixed palette

An established palette that is fixed. When a fixed palette Web browser views images, it will convert images to its colors and not use the colors from the original.

FTP

File Transfer Protocol. An Internet protocol that enables users to remotely access files on other computers. An FTP site houses files that can be downloaded to your computer.

G

GIF

A bitmapped color graphics format. GIF is commonly used on the Web because it employs an efficient compression method. See JPEG and PNG.

H

HTML

Hypertext Markup Language. The common language for interchange of hypertext between the World Wide

Web client and server. Web pages must be written using HTML. See hypertext.

hypertext

Text formatted with links that enable the reader to jump among related topics. See HTML.

I

image maps

Portions of images that are hypertext links. Using a mouse-based Web client such as Netscape or Internet Explorer, the user clicks on different parts of a mapped image to activate different hypertext links. See hypertext.

inline graphic

A graphic that can be displayed directly on a Web page. See external graphic.

interlaced GIFs

The GIF file format allows for *interlacing,* which causes the GIF to load quickly at low or chunky resolutions and then come into full or crisp resolution.

ISP

Acronym for Internet Service Provider.

J

Java

A trademarked name for a programming language invented at Sun Microsystems.

JDK

The Java Development Kit, Sun's bare-bones character-mode compiler, runtime profiler, and other tools for Java development.

JPEG

Acronym for Joint Photographic Experts Group, but commonly used to refer to a lossy compression technique that can reduce the size of a graphic file by as much as 96 percent. See GIF.

L

links

Emphasized words in a hypertext document that act as pointers to more information on that specific subject. Links are generally underlined and may appear in a different color than other text on the page. When you click on a link, you can be transported to another page on the site or to an entirely different Web site that contains information about the word or phrase used as the link. See hypertext.

live object

Netscape's term for plug-ins that enable the browser to play image, movie, and sound files as an inline component of a Web page.

lossless compression

A data compression technique that reduces the size of a file without sacrificing any of the original data. In lossless compression, the expanded or restored file is an exact replica of the original file before it was compressed. See compression and lossy compression.

lossy compression

A data compression technique in which some data is deliberately discarded in order to achieve massive reduction in the size of a compressed file.

M

MIME

Multipurpose Internet Mail Extensions. An Internet standard for transferring file nontext-based data, such as sounds, movies, and images.

O

object-oriented graphics (vector graphic)

A graphic composed of separate objects. Each object, such as a rectangle, a square, a line, or a circle, is stored as a formula called a vector. As a user manipulates the object (stretching, rotating, or resizing it), this formula is adjusted and the object is redrawn. Object-oriented graphics are created with drawing programs.

P

Portable Network Graphics (PNG)

The Portable Network Graphics (PNG) format provides a portable, legally unencumbered, well-compressed, well-specified standard for lossless bit-mapped image files. Although the initial motivation for developing PNG was to replace GIF, the design provides some useful new features not available in GIF, with minimal cost to developers. GIF features retained in PNG include indexed-color images of up to 256 colors, the serial reading of streamability files, progressive display, marked transparency portions of an image, complete hardware and platform independence, and effective 100% lossless compression. Important new features of PNG, not available in GIF, include true color images of up to 48 bits per pixel, image gamma information, and faster initial presentation in progressive display mode. PNG is designed to be simple, portable, and robust. The design supports full file integrity checking as well as simple, quick detection of common transmission errors.

Postscript

A sophisticated page description language used for printing high-quality text and graphics on laser printers and other high-resolution printing devices.

provider

Provides Internet access. See ISP.

Q

QuickTime

Software developed by Apple Computer for presentation of desktop video.

S

server

A computer that provides services for users of its network. The server receives requests for services and manages the requests so that they are answered in an orderly manner. See client.

SGML

Refers to *Standard Generalized Markup Language,* a generic text-based markup language used to describe the content and structure of documents.

splash screen

A main menu screen, or opening graphic to a Web page.

sprite

An individual component of an animation, such as a character or graphic that moves independently.

T

tag

ASCII text indicators with which you surround text and images to designate certain formats or styles.

transparent GIFs

A subset of the original GIF file format that adds header information to the GIF file, which signifies that a defined color will be masked out.

true color

The quality of color provided by 24-bit color depth, resulting in 16.7 million colors, which is usually more than adequate for the human eye.

U

URL

Uniform Resource Locator. The address for a Web site.

V

valid

In XML, refers to well-formed XML documents that satisfy the grammar defined by their DTD and all validity constraints in the XML specification.

Video for Windows

A multimedia architecture and application suite that provides an out-bound architecture that lets applications developers access audio, video, and animation from many different sources through one interface. As an application, Video for Windows primarily handles video capture and compression, and video and audio editing. See AVI.

W

well-formed

In XML, refers to whether an XML document satisfies the well-formedness constraints given in the XML specification.

WYSIWYG

Pronounced *wizzy-wig*. A design philosophy in which formatting commands directly affect the text displayed on-screen, so that the screen shows the appearance of printed text.

X

XML

Extensible Markup Language, a W3C standard for semantic and structural tagging of documents.

XML Processor

A program that reads XML documents, checks whether they are valid and well-formed, and makes their contents available to XML applications.

XSL

Extensible Style Language, an XML application for describing how XML elements are to be formatted, using either HTML or DSSSL.

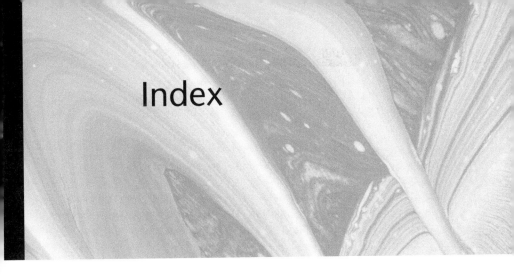

Index

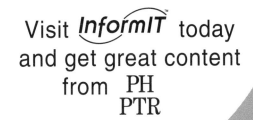

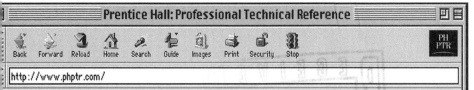